THE COLONIAL RECKONING

THE
COLONIAL
RECKONING

THE END OF
IMPERIAL RULE IN AFRICA
IN THE LIGHT OF BRITISH EXPERIENCE

Margery Perham
C.B.E., F.B.A.

ALFRED·A·KNOPF : NEW YORK

1962

L. C. catalog card number: 62–11049

THIS IS A BORZOI BOOK,
PUBLISHED BY ALFRED A. KNOPF, INC.

FIRST EDITION

TO

MY AFRICAN FRIENDS:

IN UNDERSTANDING

AND HOPE

THE LECTURES

in this book are an expanded version of the Reith Lectures given through the British Broadcasting Corporation in November and December 1961. Out of the great volume of literature on the subject, references have been given to a few works which seem especially relevant to certain points or which have lately cast some light upon the subject.

CONTENTS

THE COLONIAL RECKONING

I

Anti-colonialism
and Anti-imperialism

"Colonialism." This is a new word, or at least a word that has been used in a new way during the last few years. It is generally used in contexts which do not leave us in much doubt that it is a word of abuse. It is nearly always coupled with imperialism as if to make sure that the abuse is all-inclusive, and also, perhaps, to increase the guilt of colonialism by associating it with a word of much older and wider significance. We find these words are nearly always used in the context of an attack upon the West by most of the colonial and ex-colonial peoples. The West is a variable term. Sometimes it means the Western colonial powers; sometimes it includes the United States, or even all white non-Communist nations, with South America ranking in some contexts as an ex-colonial region. It will be seen that this division tends to put the coloured world on the one side and the white world, or at least the Western part of it, on the other.

There is no escape from the issues aroused by this attack. Only the other day I reckoned, as I put down my daily paper, that out of some thirty-eight overseas news items no less than twenty-two dealt with incidents of different kinds all over the world concerning the relations of white peoples with coloured peoples. Among these were the Congo troubles; the United States' problems in her deep South; complaints that New York hotels were discriminating against coloured United Nations staff; police raids and wholesale arrests of natives in South Africa; Afrikaner clerics pronouncing upon the theology of race relations; rebellion and repression in Angola; the Algerian war; anti-colonialist manifestations of various kinds from Indonesia, Ghana, Russia, Cuba, and Egypt; political crises in Kenya and Central Africa; the problems of West Indians in Britain. A Kurdish revolt in Iraq was ascribed by General Kassem to the imperialists, and at the outbreak of the Syrian rebellion against Egypt both sides used the same accusation, and the Russian Patriarch greeted an international conference of Orthodox clerics with a speech against colonialism.

Perhaps the bitterest expressions of anti-colonialism are those addressed over the air to coloured peoples, and especially to Africans. Anyone who wants to plumb the depths of this bitterness should study the monitoring records of the British Broadcasting Corporation. Russia, China, Ghana, and Egypt are among the centres which diffuse condemnation. Egypt—which does not share Western affection for the canine species—has much to say about imperialist dogs. The governor of Kenya, an imperialist dog, is, according to broadcasts from Cairo, bribed by the settler dogs to maintain their power over the natives. Damascus radio proclaimed that the death of Mr. Hammarskjöld, like that of Mr. Lumumba, was one of the "filthy crimes of imperialism," and China added other murders to the Western account, including that of Mr. Bandaranaike! Each advance in political emancipation by Western powers is condemned as a subtle trick to gain new kinds of control. Moscow told Africa the other day that the Americans are now "the most clever and dangerous colonialists ever known to history," and their 5,000 missionaries in Africa are "imperialists working in black garments to serve United States monopolies rather than God." At the United Nations Russia has accused the "imperialist" powers of using that institution for organizing hunger in order to get control of the wealth of the Congo. "Colonialism," another Moscow broadcast announced, "regards poverty, disease, ignorance, brutality, treachery, the bondsman's chains and the hangman's rope as its allies in Africa."

These, of course, are the extremes of propaganda. But they are intended to enlarge and exacerbate, above all to prolong, something which already exists, that great movement of assertion among the non-European peoples which has so suddenly changed the balance of forces in our world. For anti-colonialism and anti-imperialism represent the latest phase in the reaction of the rest of the world against the long domination of the West.

Professor Toynbee, in his 1952 Reith Lectures on *The World and the West* and in his *Study of History*, has put this movement into its universal setting as only he could do. He has analysed the overwhelming predominance which its technological superiority gave to the West during the last few centuries with ever increasing strength. The subjected groups have struggled to take from the West its instruments of power in order to turn them against the West, to regain their independence and to rebuild their own shaken societies. Japan showed the way with her intelligent and amazingly rapid appropriation of Western techniques. And Russia, though herself part European, felt her difference, indeed her inferiority, in relation to the West. Her leaders drew and, as Mr. Khrushchev's speeches show, still draw their main impetus from a competitive antagonism towards the West, military, economic, and ideological—the idea of communism. The coloured colonial and subjected peoples, first in Asia and now in Africa, have followed much the same lines in their consecutive dealings with the West, rejection, liberation, appropriation, condemnation. Communist China, of course, was never wholly subjected, but because of her pride in her great and ancient but isolated civilization, she reacted all the more bitterly against the string of "foreign devils" who monopolised her trade. This resentment has hardly yet found expression in action; it hangs over the West like a gathering storm.

These two attacks, the Communist and the anti-colonial, are simultaneous, and the Communist states are working hard to make them a fully combined operation. This would set some three quarters of the world against the West. This fusion has not yet happened. In the last year or so there have been developments which suggest that it may not happen. But the very possibility shows how inseparable this problem of colonialism is from the greatest of all the dangers to our world, the rift between the Communist and the Western powers.

It is upon the colonial aspect of this world situation that I want to direct our attention during these lectures. This is the part which most intimately concerns us in Britain. I should make it clear that throughout I shall be looking at the subject from the point of view of my own country. Britain has, perhaps, been more deeply affected than other imperial powers since by far the greater number of the newly emancipated peoples were in our empire. Consider for a moment the scale of the operation. Sixteen years ago we ruled some 600 million people. At the present, we are still ruling over some 30 million, and the majority of these are likely to be free in a very short time. We shall soon be left with a few small and scattered ports and islands. We may have a sense of association, even of affection, towards them, but in realistic terms some of them represent obligations rather than assets. Even the utility of some of the once cherished military bases is beginning to look questionable in this age of jets and atoms. The Britain of today is very different as regards her external power from the Britain of 1939 or even the Britain of 1945. But perhaps even more startling than the loss of governing power has been this outburst of anti-colonialism that has accompanied it. It condemns our past record; it weakens our present influence; it also threatens to harm our future relations with many of our former subjects and with other coloured peoples.

This negative anti-colonialism is to some extent the reverse side of a positive force, the desire for freedom. Our relations with most of our ex-dependencies still remain basically friendly, though this base is often obscured by clouds of misunderstanding. The real significance of the end of the Empire has been masked partly by our own increasing readiness to liberate, and also by the voluntary decision of nearly all the former dependencies, including the great states of India and Pakistan, to remain within the Commonwealth. This is certainly a matter for pride and satisfaction. But the nature of the Commonwealth is being deeply changed by this very influx of new members. Some of them are very small, none of them share the ties

of blood and culture of our earlier members, and
most of them are striking out their own independent lines in foreign policy under the general name
of "positive neutralism." Britain's proposed entry
into the European Common Market is obliging all
members of the Commonwealth to reassess the
possibility of deep changes in the nature of that
historic association. We in Britain still believe, it
seems, that it can serve both their interest and
ours, but we cannot now clearly foresee its future
shape.

In this situation of change and uncertainty
what might almost be called the cult of anti-colonialism cannot be simply shrugged off. It repre-
sents a fertile source of mistrust, especially in international affairs. Suspicion and disagreement can
grow from it overnight, as they did as a result of
the death of Mr. Hammarskjöld. It is generally expressed in something like a ritual condemnation of
imperialism which seldom shows much discrimination between past and present, between one imperialism and another, or between the different
aspects of their rule.

What has been our reaction to these events and
attitudes? People of my generation were taught
from their schooldays that our empire was a splen-
did achievement, conducted as much for the good

of its many peoples as for our own—peoples who, indeed, now owe to us the form of their existence as national states. The words "trusteeship" and "partnership" held serious meaning. To the generation before us the "white man's burden" was not a rather bitter joke. Then how, we ask, has "colonialism" suddenly, as it seems, become such a term of abuse? Have we been utterly blind? Was the idealism we so often professed merely a cloak in which we tried to hide our complete self-interest from the world, and indeed from ourselves? Has our rule really harmed these peoples, distorted or delayed their development?

In these lectures I mean to discuss these questions and others which seem to arise out of them, and in so doing to concentrate upon Africa, indeed upon British tropical Africa. One reason for this is that it would be difficult to turn to the whole colonial empire for examples. A much more important reason is that some of our largest and latest dependencies have been in Africa, and it is there that the voice of anti-colonialism is loudest. Moreover, these dependencies lie in what seems to be the world's most precarious region; its vast middle block most empty of power; its northern and southern extremities in the grip of forces seemingly irreconcilable to the rest of the continent. Further-

more, Africa makes an almost unlimited demand
for help upon the rest of the world and yet at the
same time makes any response to that demand
supremely difficult. Finally, Britain has many close
ties with this continent and has still some important decisions to make there in the very near
future.

It could be asked, and certainly the anti-colonialists will ask, whether I am going to put up a defence of colonialism. Certainly I shall attempt this
in so far as I believe our record to have been mis-
judged and to have had misleading tests applied to
it. But I hope to consider where we have failed as
well as where we have done well. Africans might
question whether someone of my nationality is
sufficiently unbiased to offer an answer to these
questions. To profess complete impartiality, as a
Chinese sage once said, is itself a kind of partial-
ity: I do not claim so much. My credentials are
bound up with my experience. Although I am
English, I have some claims to detachment. I
have sometimes worked with my government but
I have never been employed by it, and I have often
been publicly critical both of its acts and of its
policies. From the base of my university I have
been travelling in the Empire, especially in Africa,
for about thirty years, as a student of colonial gov-

ernment and of race relations. Members of my
family and many friends have been both settlers
and administrators in Africa. Indirectly my contact reaches even further back. One of my most
intimate friends and co-workers in this field, Lord
Lugard, has been in Africa since the eighties. He
in turn collaborated with the friends of Livingstone. He went himself to explore, to annex, and to
govern in tropical Africa and later, as elder statesman, to defend the interests of Africans as he saw
them. Many of my pupils in recent years have
been colonial officials coming to Oxford for re-
fresher courses after some years of work overseas.
We joined in comparative discussions of their
ideas and their work which taught me more than
they learned themselves. Many African graduate
students now come to Oxford, and a number of
these have been my pupils and friends, as have
some of the political leaders. These remarks do
not, I think, spring from egotism. I have always
believed that those who venture to pronounce
upon a controversial subject—especially with the
brevity of these talks—should explain their qualifications and what they at least think is their standpoint.

It would be well to begin perhaps by lighting
up a little the background of history to throw this

phenomenon of anti-colonialism into greater relief. We need not trace the inconstant use of the word *colony* since the time when it was used by the Romans to describe their settlements of veterans, such as that of Colchester. For of course we need no help from etymology to understand what our critics mean today by British colonialism—the rule of African and other coloured peoples by the British government or by that of our white emigrant minorities. What confuses the issue is that they constantly extend the idea from the British colonial empire to that of all European powers and slide into a denunciation of Western domination in general. They shift from past to present and even to future fears, even to what colonialism *may* do to them as it transforms itself subtly through economic intervention into neo-colonialism. It seems that not only are the Western empires to be regarded as an evil, but the very possession of economic and military power is itself to be considered discreditable. Unless, of course, this power can be put entirely at the service of the weak and poor, according to their own directions. Here the coloured peoples seem to be sharing in their own way in the escape from authority which is common throughout almost the whole world, as the bonds of family, neighbourhood, religion, status, class, and empire relax. It seems sometimes as though the only authority men will accept today, to reconstitute the ever more fluid masses of individuals, is that which arises directly from their own wills, or which can be made to appear to do so. And perhaps, of all the old authorities which are being condemned and discarded, none has fared worse than imperialism.

Here indeed is a reversal of esteem! All through the sixty centuries of more or less recorded history, imperialism, the extension of political power by one state over another, has been taken for granted as part of the established order. To appreciate the meaning of this very recent change of view we should pause for a moment and measure it against this long record.

Empire is no very exact word. It can, however, be taken to cover those dominations by which a state profited from the land and labour of other peoples. Empires were larger in space and longer in time than the little masteries that the ever shifting weight of power allowed one group of men to impose upon another. They followed, of course, an earlier stage in which men simply killed and, perhaps, ate one another. Historians judge some empires to have been mainly destructive, but many, perhaps most, in spite of their toll of suffer-

15

ing, in spite, perhaps, of being built upon slavery, seem to have been the chief means of extending peace and of spreading civilization. Certainly, if the exercise of power by one tribe or nation over another were to be regarded retrospectively as a crime, it would be difficult to find any people, except possibly the pygmies or the Eskimo, who need not plead guilty to having committed it at some time or another. As soon as tropical Africa could be observed by the rest of the world it was seen to be a vast area of tribal conflicts, of subjugations and enslavements, some, indeed, upon a sufficiently large and organized scale to qualify as the African version of imperialism.

All through the ages, it seems, men have congratulated themselves upon these extensions of their power and have gloried in exercising them. Our own Victorian grandfathers joined the chorus. Lord Milner, for instance, declared that the "Pax Britannica is essential to the maintenance of civilised conditions of existence among one-fifth of the human race." Other Victorians claimed divine sanction for the Empire. I remembered this when I was visiting the antiquities of Egypt and being wearied by the long succession of deified Pharaohs driving chariots over the bodies of their victims, or receiving long files of captives. There is one clear portrayal of the Beja people of the Red Sea, Kipling's Fuzzie-Wuzzies, being trampled into submission. So these attractive and handsome nomads felt the yoke of empire some four thousand years before they passed under the rule of Britain! And what a sequence of conquests is recorded in the Old Testament! Certainly we can see here the conquered protesting against their conquest. The exiled Israelites wanted to see the children of the Babylonians dashed against the stones. But they themselves had gloried in their own bloody conquest of Canaan and had claimed divine warrant for it. Unfortunately, this was taken by Christian conquerors of the colonial period, especially by the Elizabethan British in North America and still more by the Afrikaners in South Africa, as divine sanction for their own subjugation of the heathen.

It was an African empire, that of Aksum, out of which the modern Ethiopian empire was born, which left behind an inscription upon a marble chair, dating probably from the first century B.C. or A.D. In this the king glories in his conquest of the neighbouring mountain people and in classic terms invokes divine sanction. "I camped round about them and took what I wished of their youths and maidens and all their possessions. . . . All these peoples have been conquered by me . . .

through the grace which I have found before my august god."[1] The gods, it seemed, continued to approve, whatever the youths and maidens might have had to say.

In Rome we crick our necks gazing up at the slaughter and conquest of the Dacians spiralling round Trajan's pillar. Not far away, on the arch of Titus, we can more comfortably observe the legionaries carrying away the sacred seven-branched candlesticks of the Jews, whose captured men were worked to death building the Coliseum. The Coliseum! where thousands more, captives from colonial wars, died in various spectacular ways for the amusement of the Romans. Add to this such wholesale slaughters or sales of captives as Caesar so casually mentions in his *Gallic Wars*. A recent historian, after describing the atrocities of Rome and the vast drain upon subject populations for slaves for the mines, the galleys, the plantations, and the amphitheatres, concludes: "The growth of the empire had a background of human suffering which is unimaginable in its degree and extent."[2]

[1] M. Perham: *The Government of Ethiopia* (London: Faber & Faber; 1948), p. 22.
[2] M. L. Gordon: "The Nationality of Slaves under the Early Roman Empire," in *Slavery in Classical Antiquity*, ed. M. I. Finley (Cambridge: W. Heffer; 1960), p. 180.

Yet, because conquest led in time to the extension of peace, trade, higher standards of living, and a large measure of civic and provincial self-government, most of the peoples of the Empire settled down to contentment and even pride under its sway. Rebellion was the unforgivable sin, and the story told by Josephus of the destruction of Jerusalem makes almost intolerable reading even now. With the advent of the emperors, and the extension of citizenship, we see one great reason for the virtue men have ascribed to empires. The more lofty the seat of a ruler, the more interest he has in the welfare of *all* his subjects. It is natural that the Alexanders, the Caesars, and the Akbars of history should have favoured laws which planed down the rough uneven surfaces of humanity to an equality that provided a level and settled basis for their thrones.

The Roman Empire has therefore fared well in the reports of its contemporaries. Even the barbarians who had helped to destroy it, and the Church it had persecuted, tried to reconstruct it. Historians of the nations it subjected have associated its contribution with that of Judaeo-Christianity and of Greece as one of the three main roots of Western civilization. Some, looking back, have even regretted that the legions halted on the

Rhine because this meant that the raw tribalism of the Germans was not hammered into the same order which Rome imposed on the barbarians of Gaul, Britain, and other lands. The Roman Empire, which has so often been compared with the British, went down, certainly in destruction, and yet in a sunset of regret and remembered glory.

As we look at our own record and listen to the denunciations of our colonialism, we naturally speculate as to where Britain's policy and circumstances differed from those of this great predecessor. Was it in our briefer span of mastery? Was it that, with China far beyond Europe's horizon, Rome had no competitor, whereas Britain's empire was always one among others? Was it that Rome worked gradually, solidly outwards from her base on the Tiber, whereas Britain's collection was a miscellaneous oceanic empire in continents and islands dispersed all over the world? Were most of Rome's subjects closer to her in race? All these contrasts have some weight. But the deepest contrast of all is surely that Britain's subjects and ex-subjects have confronted her with political and, what is more, moral demands, which are new, at least in their intensity and wide acceptance. From where, we must ask, were these new standards derived? I think we shall find that, like other weap-

ons turned against the West, they have been pur-
loined from the West. And the ideal of democratic
freedom, and an almost indefinable sense of moral
obligation towards the weak, have been learned
very largely from Britain herself.

We ought not to quarrel with this. If we believe in our own principles we can hardly expect to
keep them for domestic use only. But I think we
can protest on two points. The first is that our
critics often use their weapons unrealistically and
unhistorically. Instead of regarding the element of
altruism in our dealings with them as a quite new
and difficult ideal which we have only lately
achieved in some small part, they are inclined to
judge *all* our doings and *all* our history by the latest 100 per cent standard of altruism and loudly
condemn every fall from this high grace. The reason for this perfectionism may lie partly in our
having ourselves so often and so unwisely claimed
the highest motives for all our imperial activities.
Another reason, especially for more isolated Africans, may be that not many of them have yet had
the opportunity to develop a sense of history, a
sense of the relation between time, event, and
idea, which is a rather sophisticated and largely
Western development. Tribal memories must depend more upon legend, myth, and genealogy than

upon history. Or is it, perhaps, that colonial leaders, many of them still very young, have been born into a world full of new ideas of the welfare state, of international aid, and of the need of nations today to collaborate or perish? Today we are at least *trying* to escape, through international cooperation, and especially through the United Nations, from the old law of the jungle. But this was the law which ruled international relations through all the years of our empire until the very latest, and which bound men in the dilemma between moral man and immoral society.

Another misconception arises perhaps from the use of the words "the policy of a nation." We all tend to personify nations, and colonial peoples may think of Britain in the image of John Bull or Britannia, following a dominant purpose across the decades or even centuries. Some autocracies in history have pursued a fairly consistent policy over two or three generations. The great land empires, Rome, China, Russia, the United States, could follow a clear-cut and, for long, a largely uninterrupted policy of expanding steadily outwards. But this is not true of the modern oceanic empires, certainly not of the British. No one dominant aim inspired its expansion; no government ever wholly controlled it. As soon as the vigorous, boisterous

English of the Tudor period suddenly found that the surrounding sea was not a wall, not even a moat, but a highway for their new ocean-going ships which led all over the world, they started to tumble out of their island like boys out of school. And because the highway led them and their successors at different times to many different kinds of lands and peoples, the motives of annexation and the methods of rule showed the same diversity.

Yet, for all the diversity, there were *some* dominant motives for empire. And for all the unreadiness, governments did have *some* major purposes, though these, too, shifted in character and effectiveness. It may be that, trying to look at Britain's colonial record through the eyes of her critics, we shall be able to draw up, for their benefit and our own, a very rough and ready political and moral colonial balance sheet. The critics of colonialism are mainly interested in today and tomorrow, but we must remind them that our vanishing empire had left behind it a large heritage of history which is loaded with bequests good, bad, and indifferent. This neither they nor we can easily discard.

Before we do that we must try to achieve a closer understanding of this new phenomenon of anti-colonialism. Because on its positive side it is pro-freedom, it has led in Africa alone to the astonishingly rapid emancipation since 1950 of twenty-eight states, twenty of them within the last two years, and Africans are still not satisfied with the new map of their continent. In my next lecture I want to discuss the nature of this new force and ask how it developed with such unexpected speed and power. In my third lecture I shall try to show the British response to this pressure in terms of politics, the difficult and delicate politics of bringing new states to birth. Fourthly, we must turn to consider the great and still unsolved problem of the European colonists, for this raises both the record and the future of colonialism in its most intimate, most obdurate, and indeed most tragic form. In the fifth lecture I shall offer the colonial account. This can only be my judgement, given in brief and general terms, upon our methods and agencies, our achievements and our mistakes. In my final lecture I would ask you to strain your sight by looking into the future to discern what part the ex-colonial states, which form the great majority of the so-called "uncommitted nations," are likely to play in our dangerous world, and what may be Britain's relations with her former empire.

I I

African Nationalism

In this lecture I shall try to answer the question: "What is the nature of the force that in less
than a decade has swept the rule of Europe out of
almost the whole of tropical Africa and has bred
more than twenty new nations in its place?" The
ready answer is "African nationalism." But is this
nationalism as we have known it during the last
few centuries, in the Europe where it was bred, or
is it something new? Lord Hailey preferred to call
it "Africanism," but since Africans are evoking
this force in order to create nations, we may call it

nationalism if, in so doing, we remember the special features that I intend to discuss.

A vast amount of print has been lavished upon this word *nationalism*. It has been praised for its constructive power and damned for its destructive potentiality. There have been laments that Africa should be embracing this force when the rest of the world is struggling to end it, or at least to bind it. Political scientists have long argued about the elements of which it is composed. These have been listed as the common possession of territory, history, customs, language, religion, and at least in large measure, environment and way of life. The difficulty is that some peoples have become nations though they lack one or more of these conditions. The astonishing fact is that nearly all the new African nations lacked *all* these elements except a common territory, and even that has been lately and arbitrarily demarcated by alien power. It is true that a few groups had a size and a consciousness of unity, sometimes derived from a sense of superiority, which seemed to qualify them for separate nationhood. In Africa, as in Asia, there was a tendency to claim this status just as the removal of British power threatened such groups with submergence under the majority formed by the surrounding groups. Buganda is one example, and this accounts for the difficulty of incorporating it within Uganda. Barotseland, which like Buganda had its own treaty with Britain, is another example. The Basuto developed a sense of unity from their position on the mountains and they became increasingly solid under European pressures.

For the most part, the boundaries within which Africans are now trying to form nations were drawn some sixty to seventy years ago. They enclosed hundreds, the larger even thousands, of completely independent units of all shapes and sizes. (For convenience we call all of these "tribes," although anthropologists can discern many different types of organization—or lack of it—within African groups.) Let us take Nigeria as an example. Here the British government, which had an interest in dealing with units as large as possible, felt obliged to recognize more than a hundred separate native administrations, the name given to the local governments based upon tribal groups. Language is another cause of division. There may be a dozen or more separate languages in one medium-sized country. In Nigeria there are 248. Customs are often sharply distinct from tribe to tribe. Religion divides because animist religions were intimately linked with the ancestors of each tribal or clan group, and the entry of Islam and of Christianity has in places imposed new, and often larger, divisions. Add to this the ethnic fissures, especially in eastern Africa, between Bantu, Hamitic, and Nilotic elements. There are also dramatic contrasts between ways of life. A single territory may enclose half-nomad pastoral tribes on the low, dry plains and settled cultivators on the green hillsides, divergences far greater than any that can be found in European nations, except perhaps in Russia—but then Russia is an empire! On a long day's journey by motor-car in Africa it was possible not many years ago to pass through the territory of up to half a dozen tribes, some of them still divided by a protective belt of empty, or half empty, "no-man's-land." Each might reveal different languages, forms of dress or undress, hut construction, hair styles, even agricultural methods. Today European influence tends to provide, at least superficially, an increasing degree of uniformity. Common experience enshrined in common history could exist, but the past of much of Africa is enshrined in legends, which are bound up with the heroic deeds of the founders of the parent lineage and their often shifting descendants, rather than with the total experience of a given population in a given place.

It may be said that the Asians, too, have had

their difficulties in creating truly national states. Yet they had their very large groups which shared ancient cultural and linguistic unity even though, as Dr. Toynbee has so vividly suggested, these are often dangerously mixed in a *macédoine,* or medley, rather than divided in the patchwork we see in Africa, which may in the end prove to be a safer kind of distribution.[1] Yet many of the Asian peoples had the confidence and the pride that comes from a long history, highly developed architecture and other arts, classic literature, and famous and widespread religions of the book. It is true that the ultimate origins of most nations can be traced to congeries of tribes slowly welded through the centuries. But in much of Africa the step from tribe to nation has been taken within a few dozen years and as a conscious decision.

This contrast arises, in turn, from one of the strangest facts in modern history. Here was a huge continent lying within sight of the ancient worlds of Asia and Europe. In its north-eastern corner one of the greatest of early civilizations was bred around the lower Nile, and yet its direct contact hardly seems to have spread south of the middle reaches of this great river. Africa's northern fringe

[1] Arnold Toynbee: *The World and The West: The Reith Lectures* (London: Oxford University Press; 1953), p. 74.

was much more the southern shore of Europe than its own northern border. Between this coastal belt and tropical Africa there stretched the Sahara Desert, growing ever more desiccated: a pretty formidable obstacle to full communication though never a total barrier to the passage of migration and of ideas, including that of Islam, or of trade, though this was largely in slaves. But the contact was enough to breed a succession of large states in the Western Sudan. These ancient trans-Saharan links with the world, and also the later more direct coastal contact with Europe which began in the Age of Discovery, have certainly given a long lead to the civilization of parts of West Africa, for the early Asian contacts with East Africa left little mark beyond the coastal fringe. This difference must always be borne in mind when we generalize about tropical Africa as a whole.

The great inner tropical bulk, however, still remained almost entirely secret from its neighbouring continents, shut off from direct communication with their civilizations, even very largely from their knowledge. It was long after Europeans had crossed the wide oceans to occupy the new worlds of America and Australia that they made any effective entry into inner Africa. They sailed around Africa, they occupied the temperate Cape and the

Mediterranean coastlands, and they gained footholds here and there at other points of its coasts.
But though they knew Negro slaves, since they
picked these up at the coast, they did not know
Negro-land. This was guarded by its inhospitable,
unindented coasts; by breakers and by offshore
winds; by cataracts that broke the flow of its rivers;
by desert and forest; by diseases; and also by the
apparent lack of any attractions that might tempt
Europeans to brave these multiple hostilities.

In the nineteenth century a few explorers, men
of the highest courage and resolution, began, with
heavy loss of life, the real, deep penetration of
Africa. They traced the Niger, saw the amazing
tropical snows of Kilimanjaro and Mount Kenya
and stumbled upon the great lakes. Lake Nyasa,
found by Livingstone; Uganda and the Nile source,
had to wait to the seventh decade. It was not until
1877 that Stanley emerged from the first crossing
of Africa at its equatorial girth, his hair turned
white by an expedition that took nearly three years
of terrible effort and suffering. And these pioneer
explorations meant little more than the drawing of
a few dotted lines across an empty and still highly
conjectural map.

I used to realize vividly from my talks with
Lugard about his travels that for very many tribes

the period from their first contact with the white man until today has been no more than the span of life of a very old man who could still be alive. I have once or twice myself been the first white woman to be seen by some groups, for instance in north-eastern Nigeria and on the Somali-Ethiopian frontier.

The intrusion was late but the mastery that followed was swift. The technological superiority of the Europeans insured that. Their science gave them control of disease. Their steam powered the big ships needed for the bulky produce of the tropics, and drove the trains along the rails that penetrated tropical Africa even before the roads. The first white men must have seemed almost like gods to the Africans. Much of the penetration was by consent and by rather one-sided treaties. Opposition was generally sporadic. Only in Ashanti and the Sudan was it at all serious for Britain, and to meet it there was the rifle and the field-gun, and above all, the new machine-gun, light to carry and deadly in fire-power. A few bursts and its reputation quickly spread. There was unfortunately some truth in Hilaire Belloc's couplet:

> *Whatever happens we have got*
> *The Maxim gun and they have not.*

The suddenness and the strength of his penetration meant taking over tribal Africa just as it was, almost intact, and then confronting it with twentieth-century Europe. Africans sometimes suggest that their emancipation today is the emancipation of nations which the Europeans subjected. But that surely evades the basic historical fact which explains nearly everything that has happened to Africans, that cruel trick which geography and history have played upon them and—I might almost add—upon us Europeans, who so casually took over the responsibility for their problem continent.

When at last Africans woke to self-consciousness it was to discover that as long as history recorded they had been ignored, enslaved, subjected, despised, or patronised by the rest of the world. They did not, because they could not, feel a sense of indignity as a nation, or nations. They *could* feel it as tribes, but it was more often felt by those who were already emerging out of tribalism. These felt it in two ways, first as individuals, second as members of a race. This was because in form and colour Africans, perhaps we should say Negro Africans, are strikingly marked off from other races. If to be black was to be despised, they could never escape in this life from the livery of scorn. Thus their determination to gain their freedom was altogether different from that of, say, the Greeks, Poles, or Italians who in the last century felt the shame of *their* subjection to alien rule, not so much as individuals, but rather as members of a conquered nation. Moreover, these peoples could feel themselves the equals, indeed the superiors, of the Turks, Russians, or Austrians who had subjected them. But the European rulers of Africa believed that Africans not only were almost immeasurably inferior to them in development but were inherently, permanently inferior as a race. Here lay the fundamental damaging mistake. Science and experience, and certainly my own personal experience of African pupils and friends, have taught most of us to abandon this view.

We suspect that it was cherished for so long largely because it seemed to justify the subjection, indeed the indefinite subjection, of Africans. But we need not rebound to the opposite extreme and assume that the incoming Europeans had no reason whatever for such a view, as they first explored the utter material poverty of most of Africa and tried to understand why such a vast region had remained so static while nearly all the rest of the world had in varying degrees advanced in civilization. Now, with our greater knowledge of Africa, both the old and the new, with our study of its sociology and its history, we can begin to correct this European belief in African inferiority. But there can be no doubt about the immense and lasting influence of this concept both upon European thought and therefore, in reaction against it, upon the minds of Africans.

We must think of our territories, Nigeria, Gold Coast, Uganda, Kenya, Nyasaland, Northern Rhodesia, Tanganyika, and the Sudan, to mention only the larger ones, as being, after their annexation, almost, or even entirely, passive in the hands of their new rulers. There were very occasional and very local disorders, generally almost reflex actions of individual tribes against some specific grievance. But for about the first thirty years of this century, in the western dependencies away from the coastal towns, and elsewhere for some ten or more years longer, most of Britain's new subjects lay quietly enclosed within her power, still shut off from the wider world. I travelled much in Africa between the wars, trekking widely, sometimes on horse, sometimes on foot or Model T truck, far away from centres and main roads. And yet I did not see any overt signs of discontent or antagonism; everywhere I met friendliness and eager curiosity. Colonial officials often accompanied me, but they never hesitated for a moment to let me trek and camp alone. I think that in thirty years I was only once given a police escort and that was in Kikuyu country during the Mau Mau rebellion. Only in one or two major cities on the coast of West Africa, up to about the middle thirties, did the scanty vanguard of the young politically minded define its discontents.

It looked almost like a colonial honeymoon, this period of acceptance—but not, in spite of appearances, of social health. The sinews that had held tribal life taut and virile had slackened in the wider peace and protection brought by the white man. Two acids were eating into the healthy cells of family and tribal life: the Western money economy and Christian education, both of them weakening old cultures before they could hope to construct the new.

On the economic side the new governments felt that it was both their duty and their interest, within the limited resources of those days, to do what they could to develop their parts of Africa. So, little by little, the Western exchange economy was introduced. Young men were drawn away from the village to live in labour camps or in towns, mixed with men and women, temporary wives maybe, of other tribes, and into their hands was put money. They were halfway out of the old family subsistence economy where each man or woman, boy or girl had by status an economic part to play under immemorial custom. This money was the first acid, and, where it was strong, it bit into the authority of status, so that men broke off from the clustered group and became units floating hither and thither in the open restless currents of the fluctuating exchange economy. The old men who had ruled in most of these gerontocratic little societies were often left to sit outside their huts in otiose bewilderment. The women had to adjust themselves to the new status of grass widowhood and the disruption of the family economy.

How did Africans react to these pervasive new forces? On the west coast these forces came early and penetrated slowly; and they struck many groups that were already partly immunized by long trading contacts among themselves or with the West, or by having lived in towns of their own making. Even in other parts some powers of African resilience, some capacity for adjustment, came to their aid. For the forces did not strike them all at once or all together. Some tribes took the main brunt; others were only partially and gradually affected. Many Africans learned to some extent to live in two worlds—to move from village to town and back again, even from paganism to Christian conformity and back again, or halfway back. Even so, the cumulative effect was immense, especially in those parts of East and Central Africa where the most powerful economic forces acted with great rapidity upon the smallest and most brittle tribal societies.

Most peoples in the world, not excluding the British, especially in the industrial revolution, have been through this process of the atomization of society. The break-up of the minutely cellular fabric of a society bound up with the family and close to the soil and the release of the individual into wider groupings have been the conditions of man's advance in civilization. But in most parts of the world these changes have come gradually, if with increasing speed in our century, and they have generally been to a large extent autonomous within the nation. In the colonial setting, and above all in Africa, the dissolution was caused by a sudden impact made by another race from outside. In the most exposed tribes this destroyed the environment within which their societies had been moulded. The change could bring adventure and self-development, especially to the young man. But there was also accumulated a sense of bewilderment that could burst over into a flood of discontent. This was a source of power which the new educated leaders could in time harness for political ends by pointing to the ruling power as the source of all disruption.

Next, as a disruptive force, came Western education. In many parts of Africa it had begun before annexation. In Kenya, Uganda, Nyasaland, Nigeria, to name only a few, missionaries had gone in ahead, sometimes many years ahead, of annexation and government. In what was to be Nyasaland, two Scottish missions built places of refuge and new learning in a country torn by tribal wars and Arab and Swahili slave raiding. In most parts of pagan Africa the people received them well. Very few missionaries were murdered. Their exciting novelties were often at first eagerly received —their writing and reading, their carpentry, their new crops, their medicine, even their revolutionary religious faith. They taught the Africans to play their part in building houses, schools, even cathedrals. With their many skills, the missionaries were often regarded as a great asset to a tribe. Later the governments, as in earlier days in England, left education very largely in their hands, gradually between the world wars taking over the more advanced and expensive activities.

No one thought of this education as a second acid, working side by side with the new economic forces to eat away the tissues that held together the cells of family, clan, and tribal life, elevating the book-learned child above the illiterate parent, taking him away perhaps from guarding the stock and from the circumcision school in which youth graduated in the disciplines of the tribe. He would lose respect for the ancestors and perhaps regard the religious or magical powers of the chief and medicine man as heathen superstition and polygamy as a sin. Hence the Christian schoolboy might begin to move out of his own society into a mental no-man's-land.

Western education reached much of Africa before Western economy. Before many years had passed, the schools were teaching English history, with its story of the assertion of liberties from Magna Carta to the Reform Act of 1832 and beyond. When at last the educational system reached the point when young men could go to Britain for higher education, they might meet with a deep, indeed a literally shattering experience. They were treading the road that Indian graduates had trodden before them. They realized for the first time something of the standing of their Africa in the world, or at least the British part of it. Many, perhaps most, of them would run up against the colour bar and be deeply injured by the impact. At the same time they would, in many other contexts of their new life, enjoy a sense—a conflicting sense —of freedom and equality. They would also experience a higher standard of life and an intellectual and social release that they had never known. If they were Christian, their faith might be shaken by the discovery that Britain was not the Christian country they had expected. They would learn all about the civil liberties and observe a free political life. Some of them would enter into an equal association with white women and perhaps experience what for some might be the supreme racial compensation of sexual intercourse with them. By the end of all these experiences African students might find themselves cruelly polarised between a far greater sense of racial humiliation and a far stronger determination and, indeed, hope to escape from it.

The student would return to Africa. What might he meet there? The fact of the subjection of his people to a few white officials, which he would now see with quite new eyes. He would also have the shock of seeing, again with new eyes, the poverty and, by Western standards, the ignorance of his own people. Yet had he not proved by his own

academic achievement the intellectual equality of
his race? A further blow might befall him: either
the refusal of the good official post he felt he had
so strenuously earned, or appointment to a white
man's post with inferior pay and inferior conditions. The discrimination, especially in the early
days, might have had some reason behind it. But
perhaps no single grievance has been so effective in
deepening the already deep enough bitterness of
the new intelligentsia. They might find escape
from their almost intolerable anger or sorrow by
projecting, not part of the blame, but perhaps the
whole blame, for their problems upon the white
man, and especially, of course, upon the ruling
power. It might almost be said that as a result of
all their experiences many of these young men,
these first few potential leaders, were in a pathological state of mind.

Is it surprising, then, that they began to see
only one way of escape from their intolerable sense
of personal and racial humiliation? This was to
gain independence from the white man's control,
to awaken the apparently docile masses who had
not shared their experiences and who seemed to
accept the white man's rule as part of the new im-
mutable, and perhaps not altogether undesirable,
order. They must break this spell of subjection,

then organize the new discontents into a movement for self-government, and so create a nationalism of a wholly new kind. For these young men
could not regard their haphazard blocks of Africa,
containing tribes different and even repugnant to
their own, with the emotions of a nationalist. It
was, I must repeat, as individuals, as members of a
race which was humiliated rather than oppressed,
that the masses must be aroused. The leaders
could start in the towns where men of several
tribes were thrown together in a bewilderment and
a discontent that was beginning to transcend tribalism. Today the rest of the world is seeking to
sublimate nationalism, but how else could the
Africans have sought to integrate their small
broken societies and regain their lost sense of
autonomy and dignity?

The hopes of a handful of pioneer nationalists
must at first have seemed pretty small. They still
knew little beyond the boundaries of West Africa
and Britain, and, for all their resentments, Britain
still seemed unassailable. Further, the colonial
world of the first two to three decades of this century was still, by contrast with the present, a world
of moderation. The earlier West African leaders
wanted to grow into self-government rather than
seize independence. They at once appropriated to

43

themselves the civil liberties which Englishmen had slowly wrested from the monarchy, and turned them against the re-embodiment of royal autocracy represented by their governor. They enriched their great natural powers of oratory by demanding in sonorous English the rights of habeas corpus, the liberty of the press, and any other "palladium of British liberty" appropriate to the moment. They quoted the Bible, Blackstone, Burke, and Shakespeare. They were turning against Britain her own political and judicial weapons: they were not yet making any great use of weapons manufactured outside.

Another influence internal to the Empire which fostered the growth of African nationalism before World War II was the rise of the Labour party to increasing influence, if not as yet, except for a brief spell in 1929-31, to power. The role of the Opposition in the British Parliament is far from merely negative, and for the Africans, as their awareness of what was going on in Westminster increased, the steady fire of criticism of the government's colonial policies was an immense encouragement. True, the party was at first a little confused as to the proper treatment for imperialism. It had taken to itself two historic attitudes, the philanthropic anti-slavery tradition with its positive humane interest in the welfare of subject peoples, and the much more doctrinaire and negative tradition of the old Radicals who would rather end empire than mend it. With the dawn of the century a third stream began to enter Labour thinking, derived especially from the sledgehammer attack upon imperialism by J. A. Hobson.[2] He charged capitalism, in its search for more remunerative rates of profit, with exploiting colonies and with neglecting the home market, with its lower rates for the financier but its greater scope for improving the return to the worker. This theory was later very largely undermined by economists who analysed the distribution of Britain's external investments and their rates of profit. But it was taken up enthusiastically by Lenin and worked into the Communist doctrine of economic imperialism. The British Labour party, as has often been the way in this country in the face of European doctrines, absorbed a lot of Communist thought without becoming Communist; indeed, most Western people have done the same. This theory of economic imperialism helped to confirm in the minds of colonial peoples the very natural fellow-feeling Labour had towards them, fellow un-

[2] J. A. Hobson: *Imperialism: A Study* (London: James Nisbet; 1902).

45

der-dogs who felt they had experienced much the same kind of exploitation by the capitalist ruling class as labour had.

The Labour party, however, was too pragmatic, too moderate, too British, perhaps, to advocate, even in the relative irresponsibility of opposition, the negative policy of the abandonment of an empire upon general principles, especially such a large and heterogenous empire as the British. When it came to applying a positive policy a later colonial secretary of the party declared that he did not even consider it his duty to impose Socialism on the colonies.[3] The party, therefore, groped its way to a more constructive policy, one of remedying abuses and of all-round development directed towards a gradual emancipation. Links were quickly forged between the party and native leaders in Africa and elsewhere. Some Labour members, indeed, became almost their agents, asking awkwardly well-informed parliamentary questions and raising both particular and general issues. Mr. Creech Jones, who was later to be colonial secretary, might in the middle thirties almost have been named the member representing the colonial empire and especially Africa; later, Mr.

[3] A. Creech Jones: "The Labour Party and Colonial Policy," *New Fabian Colonial Essays* (London: The Hogarth Press; 1959), pp. 21-3.

Fenner Brockway and others played the same part. Settlers, Conservative colonial secretaries, and their officials at home and overseas, were often perturbed by these constant interventions, regarding them as an incitement to disaffection. And there can be little doubt that the Labour party's activities not only guided but also stimulated the growth of African nationalism. This is not, of course, to say that the Africans were denied any such help or sympathy from the Conservative side, for neither party showed a solid front on colonial questions and the differences between their policies were mostly of emphasis rather than principle—but emphasis could be very important.

Yet Labour men could approach imperial questions with a sense of detachment, almost of innocence. I remember once flying south from Cairo with a Labour minister. At the Khartoum halt we strolled at night along the Nile, past the immense bronze Lord Kitchener, superbly confident on his charger. I wondered aloud how long it would stand, this statue we had put there. "We did not put it there," said my companion. Thus the Labour opposition could prevent colonial leaders from feeling that they were up against a monolithic opposition in Britain. On the contrary, they could find in the sympathy and moderating advice of Labour a

safety valve, which, as in India, may have prevented many reformists from turning rebels.

Beyond Britain, but still within the Empire,
Africans could begin to be aware of the spirit of
challenge in much older dependencies than their
own. As the inter-war period drew to a close, some
of the West Indians broke into riots. These evoked
the Moyne Report, which Britain withheld from
publication rather than present as valuable material for the activities of Herr Goebbels.[4] But it
was the growing strength of India's refusal to accept her dependent status or Britain's leisurely
pace for its modification which fired Africans, and
again mainly West African coastal leaders, with a
new vision of the possible. Although until quite
recently there has been little direct contact between Indian and African political leaders, *Con-
gress* has been a word of inspiration far outside the
borders of India.

The shell of colonial power was being chipped
away by more powerful forces from outside than
from inside the Empire, with great encouragement
to the African nationalism just stirring within. The
outside world had begun to impinge effectively

[4] *Report of the West India Royal Commission, Cmd. 6656, 1945*
(London: H.M.S.O.).

upon tropical Africa, and first of course upon West Africa, early in the inter-war years. This region had never been wholly isolated. Freed slaves returning to Liberia and Sierra Leone from the Americas had gone on to the Gold Coast and Nigeria with stimulating effect. The First World War had led to the recruiting of Nigerian soldiers to fight white men in the Cameroons and German East Africa. The ideas of self-determination pronounced by President Wilson reached the still scanty intelligentsia. A West Indian Negro, Marcus Garvey, based in the United States, was perhaps the first man to create an effective external dynamo of black racialism, and to plug it in across the Atlantic to the West African centres of local political consciousness. His call was for a union of all Negroes in assertion of their rights and he struck notes which were prophetic in their appeal for a racial assertion of self-respect. If white men, he said, assumed that the black man had accomplished nothing, this was because of the latter's utter dependence on the European. He even tried to found a Black Star shipping line to link the Negroes of the New World with Africa. Every race must find a home, he said, and he proclaimed "Africa for the Africans." He tried to arouse African self-respect by asserting that, when white men were apes, Africans had a wonderful civilization on the banks of the Nile.[5]

The windows that Africa opened on the world, largely as a result of the First World War, were gradually pushed further open during the inter-war years. It is difficult to overestimate the effect upon Africans, who had been largely enclosed within a bilateral relationship with their European rulers, of looking outside this enclosure and seeing themselves as part of a continent and of a world. But it was all the more exciting when it was seen that in this world events were taking place which were directly related to their own position and which showed that their rulers were not all-powerful. For almost the first time in history, the idea of imperialism had been put, however mildly, upon the defensive. Wars in our age seem to throw up a burst of idealism like a rainbow after the storm. This spirit was strong enough after 1918 to create the League of Nations. And in the Mandates System, it just succeeded in throwing a light network of status and accountability over the colonial gains of the victors. The words of the famous Article 22 of the Covenant, which spoke of peoples not yet

[5] James Coleman: *Nigeria: Background to Nationalism* (Berkeley: University of California Press; 1958), p. 190.

able to stand alone in the modern world, held a distant hint of promise. But, in so far as they heard of it, it must have seemed then a very distant promise for the African Mandates listed in the middle B category.

The years between 1935 and the outbreak of the second war were marked by two international events that were painfully relevant to Africa. Italy invaded Ethiopia in 1935. Ethiopia was one of the only two independent black states of Africa and one with an immense and romantic history. Long before Italy's aggression it had been a kind of Zion to all those Africans who had first awakened to their subjection and poverty. These were, naturally, to be found mainly in the United States, in the West Indies, and in southern Africa. They projected their emotions upon the distant, unknown kingdom, where, had they known it, Negroes were still enslaved. The cult had led to widespread, often semi-religious manifestations, which were called Ethiopianism. (Jamaica is at present the scene of a new form of this under the name of the Ras Tafari movement.) Among tropical Africans, later to awake and with less sense of oppression, there had not been so much of this sentiment. But West Africa had a vigorous press which was taking an increasing interest in African and world affairs.

Italy's lawless and cruel invasion—how well some of us can remember the horror and sense of helplessness it caused us in Britain—struck the intelligentsia deeply. The inability or the unwillingness of the other white nations to intervene turned dismay to anger. "Let Abyssinia, the only black kingdom, be shattered," cried a Gold Coast paper, "and all our hopes will be doomed." And doomed they seemed as the years ran on and Ethiopia lay crushed under Mussolini's jackboot, with her emperor a fugitive in England. Nothing is more instructive than the immediate reaction of the young Nkrumah, just arrived in London, when he saw the placard, "Mussolini invades Ethiopia." "At that moment," he writes, "it was almost as if the whole of London had declared war on me personally." He glared at each impassive face wondering if these people could possibly realize the wickedness of colonialism. "My nationalism surged to the fore. I was ready to go through hell itself if need be in order to achieve my object," [6] the end of colonialism. Here, indeed, is nationalism with a difference, an emotion aroused by the sense of common race with distant and unknown Ethiopia, an emotion in which the Londoners, distantly respon-

[6] Kwame Nkrumah: *Autobiography* (Edinburgh: Thomas Nelson; 1957), p. 27.

sible for the benign rule of the Gold Coast, seemed in some way implicated with Italy.

The rape of Ethiopia was followed by a demand on the part of the other dictator which also impinged upon Africa. Among other sops to the Cerberus of National Socialism Hitler demanded the retrocession of the ex-German colonies. Here was another and menacing anxiety for those who cared about Africa's future! For in those days of grave anxiety there were public men, most of whom have since been branded in somewhat harsh retrospect as "appeasers," who felt that perhaps the wholesale appropriation of Germany's colonies had been rather greedy and that their sacrifice might at least be preferable to another world war. There were two strong arguments against retrocession. Those of us who threw ourselves from the struggle over Ethiopia into this new controversy urged that the time had gone by when people could be handed about as pawns in the interests of European powers. But even more weighty was the fact that the sacrifice would be borne mainly by the Africans. For Hitler made no secret of his philosophy in this context and the issue quickly became entangled in ideology.

It was not only that at the time of the Peace Conference the allies had justified their retention

of Germany's colonial empire on the grounds that
her rule had been harsh and marked by a number
of cruel repressions, such as those of the Herero
tribe in South-West Africa and the Maji-Maji rebels of southern Tanganyika. There was also the fact
that Hitler was not asking for the return of the
colonies in a spirit of repentance, still less of humanity. On the contrary, her publicists were declar-
ing a new doctrine—or rather reviving one that
lay deep in some German pseudo-philosophies
which had exalted the right of a master-race, the
Herrenvolk, to rule. Britain was despised for losing
this will to rule, for betraying Nordic men, especially in what was called her feeble capitulation to
Indian politicians. "The white race," said Hitler
in 1936, "is destined to rule." [7] He claimed that
Germany was the true heir of the Roman as well
as the Holy Roman Empire. He ridiculed the weak
ideas of trying to civilize barbarous peoples or of
allowing colonies to govern themselves. In *Mein
Kampf* he had said that "it is an act of criminal
insanity to train a being who is only an anthropoid
by birth until the pretence can be made that he
has been turned into a lawyer." [8] And German pub-

[7] *The Times:* January 27, 1936.
[8] Adolf Hitler: *Mein Kampf,* Authorized Translation (London:
Hurst and Blackett; 1939), p. 359.

lic men made it clear that a rigorous policy of what is now called *apartheid* would be imposed on the Africans.[9] One result was that confidence was shaken in the mandated territories.

The main relevance to our subject of the controversy, which dragged on through 1936 to 1939, is that those who opposed retrocession emphasized the moral element in the British Empire, the policy of spreading the idea of freedom and leading towards self-government. *Our* policy, we asserted, was in absolute distinction from that of the Nazis. The Africans, and especially the West Africans, listened to this debate from the sidelines. By the time the voices of diplomacy were drowned by the guns, Britain had both advertised and advanced her promise of greater self-government for her African colonies.

The war itself deeply affected the relationship of Britain towards her colonies. Even in the First World War Britain had been forced to call upon African, as upon Indian, troops. On the whole she had obtained, both in Africa and in Asia, such support as she needed. But the Second World War was different. When Britain stood alone she was forced to ask from her African colonies not only soldiers to fight far beyond Africa but greater pro-

[9] *Völkischer Beobachter:* January 24, 1939.

duction, and very often of different goods, in return for a diminishing supply of the imported goods the Africans wanted in return. She had, therefore, to appeal for co-operation and understanding in terms never used before. There followed her defeats and colonial losses in Asia while those of her colonialist ally, France, brought enemy influence right into West Africa. Italy threatened the Sudan and actually seized British Somaliland. The relationship between Britain and her colonies could never be the same after this time of peril. On her side much of the old confidence in both military and political power had drained away: on their side they saw Britain in relation to the rest of the world with new and realistic eyes. Whether rationally or instinctively, they felt that the grasp in which they had been held had relaxed. The emancipation of India, Pakistan, Burma, and Ceylon, which followed hard on the war, was dramatic confirmation of the imperial decline—which some called fulfilment—and these events were four stars of hope to beckon the Africans forward upon their own march to independence.

By the time the war ended, the zenith of British imperial power was seen to have been, at least in part, the result of a unique opportunity, and it showed a relative diminution when her two giant allies stalked together into the international arena in their awakened strength. In its own way each Colossus was antagonistic to British imperialism.

Consider first the effect of American influence. Even in England in this war there was no moratorium upon political discussion: still less in the United States. When she finally came into the war her people knew not only that their country was *the* world power but also that *this* time there must be no retreat into isolation after the peace. The people of a nation until very recent years still in the making could not be expected to forget that her very existence as an independent state had been born out of a heroic victory over the red-coats of British imperialism. Since the war many things have combined to release America from any need to go on defining her ethos against the old British colonial image. But in the war this fulfilment had not quite been achieved. Americans felt that they were fighting a crusade for a new world, not a war to restore a damaged British Empire. Wendell Willkie flew around the world and informed it, quite truly, that it was now one. But he said something else. Everywhere, he broadcast on his return in October 1942, he found the peoples of the world loved America because she was free from the taint of the imperialism which they hated and feared.

They knew, he said, that his people stood for a different and selfless ideal.[1] The point was fully taken. Study groups all over the country discussed the coming peace, the new world order, and the end of imperialism, especially British imperialism in Asia.

A survey of the American press in 1942 would show the depth of American feeling on this point. "Quit fighting a war to hold the empire together," said the editor of *Life* in an open letter to the English people, and he went on to urge us to join Russia and America in fighting the real war.[2] America and China should come together and deal with the Indian problem.[3] Another famous writer said America must be careful to avoid being classed with Britain in Asia, and so having turned against herself "the fearful hatred of the coloured races and the blaze in their dark eyes." [4] It should be added that a few voices were raised, especially in the *New York Herald Tribune*, against the more extreme denunciators.

[1] *The Manchester Guardian:* October 28, 1942.
[2] *Life:* October 12, 1942.
[3] *New York Post:* June 9, 1942.
[4] Quoted in a letter in the *New York Herald Tribune*, February 25, 1942.

I was in America late in the war doing what little I could, not, indeed, to attack an idealism with which I was much in accord, but to try to correct distorted views of the character of our empire, especially in Africa. In the current mood it was not always easy to deal with some of my audiences. In Chicago, for example, I found that, although Queen Anne might be dead, George III was not. But the pressure of our great ally could not be ignored and I am sure that it largely increased both African hopes and our readiness to speed up the process of emancipation.

America, of course, somewhat modified her attitude before long. The other great ally turned rival did not. I must refer to this again, but let us remark here that Russian influence has played upon the Empire in three ways. First, as the theoretical attack, to which I have already referred, upon what was called economic imperialism. Second, as an example of what Communism could achieve in a huge country which resembled much of the dependent world in its industrial backwardness, in its sprawling disunity, and certainly in the illiteracy and agricultural stagnation of its peasantry. Its achievement, a real one however much it was idealized by propaganda, had a penetrating effect upon

59

peoples who had been enclosed tightly within a bilateral relationship with their rulers. Hitherto they had seen advance only in terms of following in Britain's footsteps, with Britain's help, and therefore at Britain's pace. But now Russia offered not only a condemnation of colonialism but also an alternative. Russia's third form of influence was by direct political intervention, which now had a chance to play an increasingly effective part in awakening Africa.

Finally, far more than the old League of Nations, the United Nations Organization provided a world platform from which to attack colonialism and it also established new principles and agencies with the help of which the attack could be pressed home. In the Trusteeship Council, in the Fourth, or Colonial, Committee of the General Assembly, in reviewing the affairs of all non-self-governing territories, the anti-colonial nations had a wide field on which to deploy their forces.

We have looked at the seminal ideas and emotions which gave African nationalism its special character. We have surveyed the converging events and influences which turned the world into a kind of hot-house for the forced and rapid growth of that nationalism. But we have still to see how it expressed itself in terms of politics. We have viewed it, too, mainly from the African side, and we must consider how Britain tried to deal with these strong forces, and how she ultimately handled the critical process of political emancipation.

III

The Politics of Emancipation

IN MY LAST TALK I showed, I hope, how a concentration of influences converged upon British Africa to force the growth of African nationalism. The new nationalists felt that colonialism was so oppressive that it could not be ended too quickly. Were they right? When the Belgian Congo fell almost from the day of liberation into a welter of fragmentation and murderous bloodshed, Belgium was blamed for inadequate preparation. It may be asked whether any colonial power in Africa prepared in time. It might also be asked whether the most liberal had time in which to prepare. Britain may have laid almost unconsciously some passable foundations for freedom, but it must surely be admitted that, caught by surprise, she finished off the top stories with ramshackle speed.[1]

Her long colonial history had seemed to support her estimate of African unreadiness. Her dependencies have gained their freedom in inverse ratio to their qualifications. This becomes clear if we consider the long subordination of her white colonies while they advanced step by step towards the final definition of their independence in the Statute of Westminster in 1931. Think of India, with its ancient civilization, remaining for two hundred years in association with England, before her peoples attained their dual independence in 1947. Much the same could be said of Ceylon. To accuse Britain both of delaying independence and of failing to prepare for it is to assume that she should have been preparing Africa for independence almost from the moment of annexation. But, as we saw, the colonial period covers no more than

[1] A brief account of the process, written from the inside, is given in Sir Charles Jeffries: *Transfer of Power* (London: Pall Mall Press; 1960). This is one of a number of books by the same author, a senior official in the Colonial Office, upon the Colonial Service, the Colonial Office, etc.

the span of a long lifetime. Before 1914 Britain could not begin to administer in any full sense. Her scanty agents were still making their first real contacts with the tribes, putting down slave raiding here, tribal wars and cannibalism there, building roads and railways with African labourers who in some parts had never seen an axe, a spade, or a wheel.

Then came the First World War, with two theatres of war in Africa itself, and general shortages of staff and funds. Administration, just getting into its stride, was cut to a care and maintenance basis. Hardly had Britain got again into her peace-time stride when the great slump hit the world and Africa, and staff and the budding social services were cut back remorselessly. Not until the thirties were well begun could Britain's administration of Africa really go into sustained action.

Further, Britain's equipment of experience when she began her belated administration of tropical Africa was meagre enough. The Red Indians and the Maoris had presented marginal problems, both literally and metaphorically. Britain's first real attempts at administering Africans had been in South Africa in the early nineteenth century. She had been dominated then by the strong humanitarian ideals aroused by the anti-slavery move-

ment and also by confidence in the universal ap-
plicability of her own culture. She was further influenced by philosophies about the natural good-
ness of man when left in a state of nature. These,
when presented in extreme form by Rousseau, had
prompted Voltaire to write to him: "One longs, in
reading your book, to walk on all fours." [2] These
influences, combined with inexperience, led to
what is known as the policy of "identity," of regarding men as all much the same, and so simply
extending the government and law of the existing
white colony of the Cape over the relatively few
Hottentots and Bantu within its borders. In West
Africa this policy of identity could be applied to
the small areas first annexed at the coast and con-
fusingly called "colonies." Here British citizenship
could be given, English law established, and, later,
incipient legislative and municipal councils established. The Africans were quick to respond to such
acts of faith, and it was in these politically fertile
plots that the forerunners of African nationalism
were nurtured. This policy was practicable for thousands in small coastal footholds. But what of the
millions in the vast newly appropriated interiors?
Here other methods must be found and found

[2] Bertrand Russell: *History of Western Philosophy* (London: Allen and Unwin; 1946), p. 715.

quickly. It was to meet this need that the system known as "indirect rule" was developed.

Many conquerors of peoples too numerous or too stubborn to be brought directly under an imperial government have tried to deal with them indirectly through these peoples' own authorities. Rome used client kings and allowed the difficult Jews a measure of self-government. The trials of Jesus Christ and Saint Paul show native rulers and native courts operating under the Roman power. In South Africa, when the earlier British policy of identity broke down, either in the face of numbers or because Western civilization simply did not "catch on" like some beneficent infection, Britain swung over to its opposite, the idea of recognizing that Africans and indeed other colonial subjects were *different* and could best be ruled by letting their own chiefs carry on under the general authority of Britain. This policy of limited liability and expense was applied not only to our later annexations in southern Africa—Basutoland, Bechuanaland, Barotseland—but also to the Indian and Malayan states. But, in Africa at least, it had only limited success. British authority was too detached: under it the small African society certainly survived. But without the virile challenge of independence, without active help in adjusting to new conditions, the native system grew weak or corrupt.

Indirect rule was tried out, therefore, as a much more dynamic and rationalized version of this policy. It was first applied by Lugard in the advanced Moslem city-states of Northern Nigeria. With his derisory resources of men and money he had no option but to incorporate these effective native governments almost as they stood. But he was the first to see that the incorporation must be made fully active, must link the native systems closely with the British administration. He adjusted his system carefully to fit all types and sizes of African society, from the princely states with hundreds of thousands of subjects all the way down to little pagan clans, defining the exact measure of administrative and judicial authority appropriate to each.

The experiment was at first spectacularly successful. Lugard was a very thorough man and his lavish documentation in laws and instructions, and later his classic, *The Dual Mandate*,[3] helped to dif-

---

[3] F. D. Lugard: *The Dual Mandate in British Tropical Africa* (London: W. Blackwood; 1922). I have discussed indirect rule fully in my biography of Lugard, especially in Volume II. M. Perham: *Lugard: The Years of Adventure,* Vol. I, 1956, and *The Years of Authority,* Vol. II, 1960 (London: W. Collins).

fuse his model. Administrators of his own school were promoted to important posts in Africa and beyond and carried his principles with them. During the thirties almost everywhere in British Africa I found "indirect rule" was the gospel. Even today nearly all British Africa still bears the imprint of this system.

It certainly had its merits. It broke the shock of Western annexation; it was economical; it kept the peace; and it induced a sympathetic, inquiring attitude in colonial officials towards African society. But too much success can crystallise administration: in lesser hands means can become ends—dead ends. There was a tendency to warp and discredit chieftainship by making it too much the agency of alien power. And while at best the system could and did reform and modernize native societies, at worst it could stereotype them.

If the principle behind direct rule was that of identity, the principle behind indirect rule was that of differentiation. Certainly the vast numbers of newly annexed Africans *looked* different enough from Europeans. But they were not inherently, permanently different. They could change. It was here that the system tended to become static. In theory it was like a steel framework, fitted with interstices carefully made to accommodate native societies of all shapes and sizes under over-ruling British powers. But almost from the first the grid failed to remain all-inclusive. Individuals were drawn out of their societies, drawn to the new central government, to wage labour, to work in offices, to the growing towns. For while with one hand government was trying to preserve and control tribal society, with the other it was opening Africa to economic and other forces which were bound to undermine it. In the thirties these socially and politically displaced persons showed their discontent with indirect rule. Whenever I talked to educated Africans their constant themes were that it led nowhere and had no place in it for them.

Generally, the thirties and forties covered a period of gradually accelerating reform. All departments moved forward, and some of the moves had political content—the development of trade unions, of co-operative societies, of the community, of higher education. The Colonial Office itself was enlarged and adjusted to new and wider tasks. But none of these reforms could satisfy the West African élite, for none of them offered an adequate answer to their own immediate ambitions or to their great new hopes about the political future of their territories. Speeches and leading articles in the local press steadily increased the strength of their denunciations. In Nigeria and beyond, Dr. Azikiwe, in his *West African Pilot*, was both leader and model. His deadly use of ridicule was aimed at destroying the dignity and prestige of officialdom.

It was in the Gold Coast that British Africa's first Negro state was born into independence. The story is told with subjective vigour in Dr. Nkrumah's autobiography. The full complement of almost ritual acts is there—the leader's return from education overseas; the organization of a party; the appeal to the masses; the attempts by government at private parley; the uncompromising demands; the sloughing off of the moderates and the formation of a wider, more resolute party; the growing threat of force; the disorderly incidents, the imprisonment of the leader; the Commission of Enquiry. Because the leader was in a British prison, he was given facilities to enable him to stand in a general election. He was, of course, elected, and there followed his immediate release and assumption of power. Dr. Nkrumah had made an exact estimate of the strength of the fortress confronting him. It had become as light as a stage property. Two or three pushes of his strong, irreverent hands and it was over. And on the other side was the governor, Sir Charles Arden Clarke, "a tall, broad-shouldered man," writes Nkrumah, "sun-tanned, with an expression of firmness and discipline, but with a twinkle of kindness in his eyes," who "came towards me with his hand outstretched." [4] Shortly after this, I was able to stay with Sir Charles and observe the close and friendly co-operation in which he and Dr. Nkrumah worked to prepare the Gold Coast for independence.

The events I have described could not have happened just like this in 1939. The war and all those resultant influences which I discussed in the last lecture had subtly changed Britain's attitude, though perhaps the authorities hardly knew it until they were faced with the decision. The final responsibility rested, as always, on the chief man on the spot. Asked once whether he had telegraphed the Colonial Office before letting Nkrumah out of prison, Sir Charles frowned a little, as if with the effort of trying to remember, and then said: "I can't remember." A good revealing reply!

The emancipation of the West African states presented fewer problems than those which face Britain in East and Central Africa. But in the conditions of Africa, although each territory had its own very individual character, and therefore its own route to freedom, most liberations have been hazardous hit-and-miss transactions which have

4 Nkrumah: op. cit., p. 137.

thrown an almost intolerable strain upon all concerned.

Consider the Africans' side. The leaders are
generally young graduates. They are often inexperienced in politics, and nearly always in administration, which most of them take for granted, expect-
ing it to continue its basic functions whatever the
politicians do on their level. They are newly infected—as I tried to describe in my last lecture—
with a fever of indignation about their individual
and racial status. "My country groans," said Dr.
Azikiwe in 1948, not—as you might expect him to
add—under this or that substantial oppression but
—I quote again—"under a system which makes it
impossible for us to develop our personalities to
the full." I remember the tone of voice and flash
of eye with which a young leader from French Africa exclaimed to me: "*You* have never known
what it is to live under colonialism. It's humiliating." It is, indeed, difficult to exaggerate the state
almost of "possession" felt by African leaders during their struggle, as they awoke to their status. At
a critical moment in Uganda one young politician
confessed to a European friend that he could
hardly get near to a white man without wanting to
stick a knife into him. To quote fragments from

Africans from French territories, who reveal the alien influence by writing in verse—French verse:

> *Afrique dis-moi Afrique*
> *Est-ce donc toi ce dos qui se courbe*
> *Et se couche sous les poids de l'humilité.*

Again:

> *Les vagues furieuses de la liberté*
> *Claquent claquent sur la Bête affolée*
> *De l'esclave d'hier un combattant est né.*[5]

Monsieur Léopold Senghor, President of Senegal, and a distinguished poet, writes:

> *Je n'ai haï que l'oppression . . .*
> *Ce n'est pas haïr que d'aimer son peuple.*
> *Je dis qu'il n'est pas de paix armée, de*
> *   paix sans oppression,*
> *De fraternité sans égalité. J'ai voulu tous*
> *   les hommes frères.*[6]

[5] David Diop: *Coups de Pilon* (Paris: Présence Africaine; 1956), pp. 14 and 21.
[6] Léopold Sédar Senghor: *Éthiopiques* (Paris: Éditions du Seuil; 1956), p. 40. From " 'Chaka,' aux martyrs Bantus de L'Afrique du Sud."

73

Such intensity of feeling was not confined to Africans. That so moderate and all-comprehending writer, Nirad Chaudhuri, relates how, as he sat in the balcony at the opera in Calcutta, looking down at the well-dressed English audience in the orchestra, he was seized with such a ferocity of hate that he longed to drop a bomb and kill them all. He adds that there could be no redemption for India until it could escape from the "snake's fangs" of such hatred,[7] and, indeed, thank God, it seems to be making this escape.

To return to our African leaders, they had to be men of great powers of self-assertion. Confronting them were all the positive forces of the established colonial order, with its supporting tribal authorities, and the negative passivity of the masses. They had to construct their own platforms and jump upon them. They had to create parties by which to communicate their own assertive indignation first to the towns and then to the tribes. Their resources were often very small. Their movements had often been born abroad—mainly, for British Africa, in London. Here students from different territories could stimulate each other and find sources of European support and encouragement.

[7] Nirad Chaudhuri: *Autobiography of an Unknown Indian* (London: Macmillan & Co.; 1951), p. 420.

They certainly came up the hard way. Dr. Nkrumah tells us how in London he and his friends—probably in clothes of inadequate warmth—would work in a little office so cold that their breath fogged the one electric light, and how they would walk for miles at night picking up bits of coal fallen from carts and around coal-holes.[8] Back in Africa it was hard enough. There would be almost no regular funds; a cheap office or two in the capital might be rented as party headquarters: there would be little equipment or trained staff: excited young Africans would crowd it out. In the bush the party's branch office might be in a hut, with not always the most intelligent or scrupulous agent in charge of it. The party would hardly be formed before it would be demanding self-government—and at once! Their cry was like the Red Queen's: "Faster. Faster," and, in British eyes, almost as unreasonable. Why such haste? Because of the head of psychological steam which had been raised behind the movement and which had to be sustained. Because nearly every African leader was—and is—constantly in danger of being outbid and therefore outflanked by a rival leader. Even to name a date for independence was to be discredited by a claim for an earlier date.

[8] Nkrumah: op. cit., p. 55.

75

I have been in six African states during their crises of transition and my recollections turn from the excited African side to the apparent calm of the governor's office. The governor's first duty must be to maintain public order. His entire staff, from the senior officials down to every hard-pressed officer precariously out in the bush, every African chief, or elder, every policeman, draws its authority from the governor and looks to him to maintain the established order against those "angry waves" of the poet which beat against it. It may be official policy to make orderly and gradual concessions. But very often that does not suit the African leaders. They need to strike the defiant posture of demanding, of taking, never—this is surely understandable—of appearing to *receive* their freedom. The governor may have genuine fears for minorities. He knows that working out a new constitution and the first registration for universal franchise takes more than a matter of months. Meanwhile the pressures rise. Is he to stand aside and, in some territories, see the moderate, the loyal, or even the indifferent, intimidated; their houses burned, perhaps; the law flouted; the economy halted? He may remember all that followed Amritsar and will allow no shooting except as a last resource. The leaders know this and on their side

may court arrest. Had not Dr. Nkrumah, with prec-
edents from India, shown that graduation through
prison was an almost essential distinction for a
leader?

During the fifties—this last decade of agitation
and achievement—the incitements, which had
done so much to ignite the fires of nationalism,
could be used to blow upon the flames. Dr. Nkrumah's Ghana was no static symbol of enfranchisement: it was a power-house from which radiated
currents to increase the power and heat of nationalism elsewhere. The 1955 Bandung Conference of
twenty-nine Asian and African states was the dramatic prelude to a series of meetings, mainly in Africa and especially in Accra and Cairo, at which
Egyptians, Ghanaians, Tunisians, Moroccans, and
perhaps Russian and Chinese, could give leaders
still under colonial rule advice and, more than that,
the sense that victory was within their grasp. A
leader might go abroad to Ghana, Cairo, the
United States, even to Moscow or Peking, to gain
the support and confidence he needed in order to
face official opposition at home.

Perhaps the most serious problem of the transfer was due to Britain's tardiness in opening the
civil service to Africans. The new African leaders
needed a service in which loyalty and enthusiasm

counted more than efficiency. The governor, on his side, in this crisis of confidence needed the utmost steadiness and devotion from all his staff, and this at the moment when they were being faced with the abrupt end of their careers. They might, of course, have the option of signing on for a period under new masters, those men, perhaps, who seemed to have been condemning all they had done and all they stood for. Would these, they questioned, have the constancy, or indeed the resources to honour their engagements, and especially to resist the thrust of young supporters eager for promotion? Would they honour the principles of political impartiality of the civil service, when possibly impartiality was the last thing the new government party was asking—or needed?

The more experienced African leaders would confess to their great need of expatriate staff and would even offer public appeals and public thanks to those who were leaving. On its side, the British government hesitated almost to the last to give the full assistance and assurance which could have eased the crisis for both sides. The marvel is that so many officials have stayed and worked so well, and for this both they and their African employers can take great credit.

What happens on the morrow of independence? The new states set out as parliamentary democracies with universal suffrage, with all the human rights and civil liberties in their constitutions. Very soon most of them depart from this. The Sudan and Pakistan have passed under military rule. Democracy in Burma and Ceylon has, to say the least, been shaken. Ghana has made a dramatic break with the full parliamentary democracy, complete with an opposition, with which she started, and has developed a one-party state under personal —very personal—rule.

A moment ago we looked at African leaders as they struggled for power. Now put yourself in the position of one of them as he succeeds to that power. He belongs to a very small educated élite; a vast gap yawns between this and the illiterate masses which had rallied around him for a single, unifying purpose, driven by the impulse, more of emotion than reason, to free themselves from subjection to foreign rulers. This achieved, they would tend to fall back either into their tribal groups or else right out of them into a bewildered mass demanding re-integration under strong, even dramatic leadership. The leader must retain the élan and unity of the independence movement, and the simplest method of doing this is to beat the familiar defiant note on the national drum—the anti-colonial note. This is one of the oldest devices for deflecting potential discontent and disunity away from a government and on to some convenient enemy. It arouses that aggressive instinct which can be the strongest bond of a group. But the leader also needs positive support, an emotion which can transcend other emotions, especially that of loyalty to chief and tribe. To these socially orphaned people he must exploit his personality until he becomes, the psychologists might say, the super-self or the father-figure. We are driven to use the fashionable adjective charismatic, the charism on the leader's brow, an anointment which must be made to seem not quite of this world.

In addition to maintaining their newly created hold over their own people, there are other demands upon the new leaders almost beyond human capacity to meet. The ministers have to undertake the new discipline of long hours of arduous office work. In a world of over a hundred nations the greater part of these seem determined to visit or to be visited. There are a score of conferences at home and abroad, including the great and all-important conferences at the United Nations. Prestige demands a number of expensive, complicated, and not always remunerative gestures—a huge stadium, of course, is a first essential, but so also are a national airways, a fleet, television, a steel mill, a harbour, a hydro-electric scheme, impressive state buildings, government offices, and ministerial houses. Delegations of businessmen and contractors arrive in streams. There are all the temptations for corruption. A little corruption may oil the joints of a stiff new machine, but too much of it clogs the works.

Opposition to this busy new government may be based not upon any political principle but upon sectional, even separatist, ambitions. Is this opposition, the leaders may ask, to be given a chartered liberty to disrupt, to entrench disunity, even to threaten to replace their new hard-working governments, and the party which has won independence? In these circumstances, government by debate may seem too difficult and government by *diktat* too easy. In the amorphous condition of some newly independent colonies the ruling party is not only the sole party; it has very largely been the creator of the new independence and is almost indistinguishable from the state. This is especially true of Tanganyika and may prove to be true of Nyasaland.

In past history, we may reflect, peoples won freedom under great leaders, not shadow cabinets: independence and parliamentary democracy did not necessarily go together. Why did Africans combine them? Partly because our system was, at least in the past, the most admired and enviable. But it also offered them the warrant for independence. Universal suffrage provided the perfect means of voting Britain out on Britain's own principles. Why did we on our side agree to equate colonial independence with the Westminster model? The American presidential system, with its separation of powers and its fixed terms of office, might have ensured more stability. But we could give only what we had, what we knew. Certainly, in the earlier transfers, if we had offered something else labelled "Made for Africans," it would have been rejected as insulting.

In so far as Africans may depart from our form of democracy, the reasons will lie not so much in African incapacity as in African conditions, and, indeed, in conditions far beyond Africa. If we took a map of the world and coloured the states that are genuine democracies we would get a pretty blank design! The Westminster model is the end result of at least two thousand years of national development in a highly favourable island site. Africans are attempting almost the exact reverse of our British experience. First we had a coagulation of our separate tribes and kingdoms. Then some centuries of development of a central government by kings who presided over an increasingly united people and hammered dissidents into shape. Then the control of government passed by stages from the king to the nobility, to the gentry, and to the new middle classes bred by the industrial revolution. Finally, with the diffusion of a high, and relatively to other countries an equal, standard of living, and of universal education, we at last achieved our present full democracy. Africans have taken over this end product before any of its necessary antecedents have been achieved.

Africans know this argument well. They will expect it to end with the conclusion that they should have remained under tutelage for another two thousand or at least two hundred years. This is *not* my conclusion. I want to state with all emphasis my belief that once Africans had been fully stirred into racial self-consciousness and political awareness, prematurely though this may be in their own interests, there was little more that foreign rulers could do for them. We may try to equate Ghana with the Tudors or the Congo with the War of the Roses. But our immensely gradualist history cannot be exactly fitted to theirs. They feel that they need, and can now borrow, quicker if more dangerous mechanisms of change that may in part

83

—only in part—make up for their lack of wider unity and experience. What should be Britain's attitude to such new dictatorships? Should we merely express our disappointment? Or should we remind a constitutionally defaulting state of the democratic liberties which are the greatest bond that holds our Commonwealth together? Its leaders may remind us that whatever fractions of democracy we allowed them, the basis of the colonial states was autocracy. How are we to sympathize with our friends when they are wrongfully exiled or imprisoned? It is clear that any criticism from Britain can touch the anti-colonialist nerve so painfully that dictatorship may harden in response and look elsewhere for example and support. Yet, if we are silent, are we not denying our political faith? Indeed, Chief Awolowo has declared that any Western tendency to excuse deviations from democracy is only another insulting colonialist assumption that Africans are too primitive and barbaric to conduct what he calls "this beneficient and ennobling form of government." [9] True, he is the leader of the opposition in Nigeria's federal parliament. But he is also a practical ruler who as Premier of the rich Western Region did much to

[9] Obafemi Awolowo: *Awo* (Cambridge: Cambridge University Press; 1960), p. 302.

construct an impressive welfare state, in which an opposition, if it has its difficulties, is at least able to exist. It seems, therefore, as though Britain will encounter criticism whether, in the face of deviations from democracy, she shows disapproval or refrains from it.

The achievement of independence in Africa must always be a precarious adventure. I have suggested some of the reasons for this. Ghana, of course, has given her friends in Britain most cause for anxiety. But the Sudan has also had its problems. The leaders of the Anglo-Egyptian Sudan were able to force the pace of emancipation less by an appeal to the masses than by using the status of their country, a condominium of Britain and Egypt, to play her co-rulers off against each other. The sophisticated dark Arabs of the three towns which cluster round that dramatic meeting place of the Blue and the White Niles were well able to provide leadership for this political struggle. Perhaps nowhere in any dependency in the world had relations between colonial ruler and ruled been more harmonious, more full of mutual respect, and nowhere had the more selfish ends of empire been less in evidence. If the transfer of power took place too quickly, in the view of our officials, it was achieved, in the main, harmoniously. The Sudan was one of the regions of Africa where I had spent my most congenial hours of study and travel. I was able to be present at some of the constitutional discussions presided over most benignly and ably by Sir James Robertson, as civil secretary. I shall have a few words to say in my next lecture about the degree of preparation given to the Sudanese for independence. Here we must note that they started off with a fully British-type constitution, for which they hurriedly constructed a building on the plan of the House of Commons. Their subsequent relapse into military dictatorship—of a fairly mild kind—was caused less by the breakdown of the constitution from internal causes than by the danger that their ambitious neighbour, Egypt, might exert her wealth and influence upon inexperienced M.P's to bring in a pro-Egyptian party.

Ex-British Somaliland gained independence, in spite of the poverty and inexperience of her semi-nomad population, because the United Nations had named a date for independence for her neighbour, Italian Somaliland. The British government, though well aware that her Somalis, for all their high individual courage and intelligence, were anything but ready, collectively, could not, in these circumstances, propose any further delay, though it was realized that the new Somali nation would take over a heavy burden of poverty, inexperience, and dangerous frontier problems. The promised emancipation of such unready peoples proved a strong argument in the hands of those other Africans who could rightly claim to be more ready.

As each territory gains independence, the volume of precedent accumulates to hasten further emancipations. Thus Sierra Leone, in spite of the small size of its territory and the rift, now rapidly healing, between the long-Westernized, ex-slave people of the coastal fringe and the long-isolated tribes in the hinterland, strolled quietly into nationhood late in 1961 in an atmosphere of the utmost good will and mutual congratulations between her leaders and Britain.

Tanganyika had not only a heavy volume of precedent behind her to carry her smoothly forward to the celebrations of December 1961. It had also the status of a Trust Territory under the United Nations, and its destination was obvious almost as soon as it came to be seriously discussed. Even so, there is no more instructive illustration of the power both of external pressure and of precedent than the way in which leisurely plans for self-government, which would also have preserved

87

a place in the constitution for the European and Indian minorities, were pushed forward with ever increasing speed to the culmination of complete African majority and one-party rule. Part of the reason for this breathless advance may be found in the characters both of the governor, the realistic Sir Richard Turnbull, and of the then Prime Minister Mr. Julius Nyerere, certainly the most poised, confident, extroverted, and indeed radiant of all the African leaders I have met. Yet Tanganyika will not easily become a nation.

I have reserved Nigeria to the last. From the moment that Dr. Nkrumah forced the pace for his less than five million people it was obvious that Britain would not refuse Nigeria's thirty-five millions their independence. It is of great importance, not only to the Nigerians but to Africa as a whole, that this its most populous state should grow in strength and unity. Its achievement of eminence in world affairs would be the best of all satisfactions for the Africans' hunger to assert the dignity of their race. The leadership, at least of independent Negro Africa, is there for Nigeria to take. But such a new combination of disparate parts, brought together so recently by an external power, has still to be cemented by leadership and common experience.

Three major groups inhabit the three regions. They are the proud conservative Moslem Hausa of the north, with their ancient city-states; the Christian, Moslem, and pagan Yoruba, also proud of their long history and also having large cities but being as a people much more Westernized; and thirdly, the Ibo and kindred tribes of the southeast. These last were a people who knew no chieftainship but who make up for any political and cultural handicaps by their intelligent energy, and who pour out of their overcrowded forests to compete with other tribes all over Nigeria and beyond. These three sharply distinct groups could each, in size, resources, and cultural unity, have qualified better for separate nationhood than many other of the new African states. It was not easy, as the bonds of British power which held them together loosened, to devise a constitution that would hold them together in free and effective co-operation. Yet it was difficult, as Ghana forged ahead in the race for independence, to ask Nigeria to be patient.

Fortunately it proved possible, during the ten years following 1950, for the British government to work out the pattern for Nigeria's future step by step in the closest collaboration with the African leaders. The only bloodshed, at a very early stage, was the death of a few striking coal-miners who took possession of some dynamite, and the nationalist leadership had to make the most of the incident.

The constitution, which was gradually hammered out in a long series of very full conferences in London and Nigeria, worked towards a system that would give the strong regional forces a very large measure of self-expression in regional governments, while the whole country was held within a federation. The regional governments attained their independent status first. Thus, when federation came, there were many Nigerians with experience of office who could staff both federal and regional ministries. The southern Nigerians chafed at the slow progress. For this they blamed the north, which was too conservative to be hurried but far too large and important to be overridden, still less to be left out. The governor-general, Sir James Robertson, presided over the last stages of the transfer of power, gradually easing the ministers into their new responsibilities, the last to be handed over being security and foreign affairs. Although the Nigerians were sometimes indignant at the delays and from time to time struck the old anti-colonialist attitudes, the whole delicate operation was carried through with an astonishing amount of good will. When it was over, some of the ministers readily admitted that their new nation had gained greatly from the ten years of gradual preparation.

I do not propose here to discuss the form of the constitution. It is enough to say that, with allowance for the federal character, it follows the lines of the British system and is supported by the civil liberties, including the independence of the judiciary, while civil service commissions have been set up to protect the civil service.

It is too soon yet to say whether the constitution will hold Nigeria together in a progressive unity. The different, and in some ways opposed, groups, though they find some healthy self-expression in their own regional politics, are still in some ways mutually antagonistic. In each region, especially along the southern border of the north, there are minority groups that tend to make their protest by supporting the dominant party of another region. This produces an opposition within the regional assemblies, but not of the most healthy kind. Meanwhile, at the federal level, the mainly northern and south-eastern parties have made a coalition, while the western Yoruba party, the Action Group, forms the opposition. Here, again, it would not be healthy if what is in the main the party of one region were to be permanently in opposition. Yet the large and conservative north tends, by its alliance, to steady the almost over-energetic Ibo party, and the Ibo governor-general, Dr. Azikiwe, has lately praised the efficiency of the emirates, which he and his former party tended to regard as too autocratic.

The federal constitution to some extent inhibits Nigeria's speed of action and mutes her voice in international affairs. No one group can freely express its spirit at the national level and no one man, not the Prime Minister, even if he wished, could exercise anything like the dynamic and uninhibited leadership of a Nkrumah. This is prevented by the distribution of federal ministries among members of the different regions and by the existence of three regional governments with strong premiers. For a people still inexperienced in modern government and especially in international affairs, this may seem a healthy restriction. If this delicately balanced trinity can be maintained for a few more years, it may become more stable. One great need is that the proud emirs and ruling class of the north should open their long isolated citadels of power to the incalculable forces of democracy.[1]

In the present stage the country owes much to the ability of the three regional premiers and the Prime Minister, and it may be hoped that Nigeria is now so strong that it will not find Western appreciation the kiss of death, or even of detriment. The Prime Minister is eminent for his dignity, patience, and high principles. He has the true *gravitas* of the statesman. He has even the courage to disclaim much indulgence in those fashionable "isms," anti-colonialism and anti-imperialism. Nigeria gained, as did India on an even vaster scale, from having leaders who had established their reputation long before the coming of independence; men able to withstand, at least in some measure, the pressures of the inexperienced and the impatient.

Nigeria has a geographical advantage in the solid square of her territory, which has a rainfall allowing it to maintain, by African standards, a large and well-distributed population. Its great river, the Niger, with its tributary the Benue, trisects the country; and the colonial government

[1] For a description of the making of Nigeria's constitution see K. Ezera: *Constitutional Developments in Nigeria* (Cambridge University Press; 1960).

93

leaves behind it a system of communications which helps further to bind the country into one economy. But the great political bond for Nigeria will be the knowledge that only through unity can it claim, and keep, the leadership of tropical Africa.

I have dwelt a little upon the problem of Nigeria to illustrate the difficulties that have faced Britain and her colonial peoples over the transfer of power. One of the difficulties, however, is that Nigeria is by no means typical. There is no type. Each African dependency, like all the others, is unique and has presented wholly different problems both in politics and in the techniques of making a constitution. No Colonial Office department has been so overworked as the legal department, which handles the intricacies and varieties of constitution-making. To the outside world the emancipation of a colony may seem little more than a large, sweeping, rapid, and overdue gesture —although since the Congo disaster this view may have been modified. But only those who have seen the process at close quarters can grasp its difficulty.

There are two ways of approaching the problems of colonial emancipation. One starts from the point of long distance and asks whether Britain foresaw at a sufficiently early date the direction events were taking and made the necessary major preparations for their advance. This question I shall discuss in the fifth lecture as a part of my general assessment of the British record. In the present lecture we have considered the other aspect of the process, the final concentration of African nationalism into a demand for immediate self-government. In reviewing these events it appears that nowhere, except in regions of white settlement—the subject of the next lecture—did Britain even attempt to refuse the demand once her government was convinced of its strength. The problem was essentially one of timing. With British standards of efficiency and sense of obligation to minority groups, the colonial governments wanted the transfer of power to take place by gradual and orderly stages. At one time they had visualized a period of responsible self-government before independence, which, they had assumed as a matter of course, would be within the Commonwealth. It was the African leaders who, making full use of that changed balance of forces which I discussed in my second lecture, forced the pace. I was often amazed, in discussing the subject with these often quite young and politically inexperienced men, at the apparently complete self-confidence with which they contemplated taking over the responsibility for a new African state, in all its unreadiness and poverty. Nearly every time-table for advance was progressively shortened: constitutions framed for five or seven years would hardly last for two. One reason for this could only be learned by hazardous experience. This was that power cannot be held in suspense. Once it was known that power *would* be transferred, the position of the colonial government might become so weak, and that of its still irresponsible successors so strong, that the interim period of uncertainty would be intolerable, if not dangerous. It is some cause for congratulation to both sides that so far Britain has nowhere simply abandoned her last difficult responsibilities, and that no African leaders have cut short the trying period of transfer by reaching out for power with lawless hands. But the most difficult tests, those of the territories of white settlement, are still to come.

I V

The Problem of
White Settlement

I MUST CONFESS that I have found it rather difficult to hold the question of white settlement for
this talk. Much that I have been saying about
African nationalism and British policy applies also
to the settled areas of British Africa. There is one
fundamental difference. A British government can
just pack up and go when the moment for abdica-
tion arrives. But where there is a hard stratifica-
tion of white minority over black majority and the
black layer begins to heave into political assertion,
the whole structure threatens to disrupt. Consider

the map and the areas of conflict in Africa. Algeria—a million settlers, six years of war. The cost? Perhaps 200,000 lives—so far! Angola—thousands killed by African massacre and by Portuguese repression. The Congo—a chaos from which thousands of Belgian settlers have fled. Kenya and Central Africa? They now face Britain with her gravest remaining problems. South Africa? Three million whites in a rigid stratum still holding down 10 million Africans.

The total population of Africa can only be estimated, because African conditions make exact enumeration difficult and some countries have never even attempted a proper census. The total is estimated at about 242 millions. This includes some 235 million Africans and some 5½ million Europeans: that is, less than three Europeans to every hundred Africans. The great majority of the Africans are the Negro or Negroid peoples south of the Sahara barrier, with the Arabs, Berbers, and others to the north. But this barrier is being increasingly crossed, physically by airways, politically by the new unities of anti-colonialism. The two Rhodesias, still reasonably temperate, accommodate some 300,000 settlers. But even in their main strongholds of Algeria and South Africa the whites are only a minority. Between these two regions, which are some 3,000 miles apart, are scattered the remaining half million Europeans. The greater part of these scattered whites are birds of passage, government servants, businessmen, missionaries, and so on. Even in Kenya a very large proportion of the 65,000 whites are not rooted settlers.

Africa is, therefore, pretty solidly African. How is it, then, that the small numbers of Europeans do not represent a small problem?

Most of the world's nations are amalgams resulting from migrations and mixtures. Many circumstances have helped the process of fusion. There was generally time, plenty of time, for gradual integration. But the modern domination of the world by the West was accompanied by migration of a new and powerful kind. The migrants came across the oceans from an utterly different civilization. They came abruptly in their ships, with all the power of their new weapons and new techniques, above all with the strength which resulted from their retaining contact with their base in Europe. Crowded, industrious Asia offered them no foothold for settlement. But in South and North America, in Australia and New Zealand, the white immigrants found scanty, ill-distributed peoples and these they dominated and either displaced, destroyed, or decimated. The newcomers then quickly proceeded to build their own utterly different civilization. But since these new migrants were rationalizing people, they had to make out a case for their actions. Gilbert Murray has drawn attention to such claims in a striking exaggeration. "Unnatural affection, child-murder, father-murder, incest and the violation of the sanctity of dead bodies—when one reads such a list of charges against any tribe or nation, either in ancient or modern times, one can hardly help concluding that somebody wanted to annex their land." [1]

That most of the peoples whom the Western colonial nations conquered were coloured was accidental, a very unfortunate accident, as time was to show. Among the most horrible illustrations of Gilbert Murray's remark was the behaviour of the Spanish conquerors of the lonely empires of Mexico and Peru. In the Age of Discovery most of the discoverers were men of violence. So here was wholesale plunder, slaughter, and enslavement of the peoples of these fascinating but fragile civilizations. Yet, for the first time in history, colonialism had to meet the challenge of Christianity. A great Christian, Las Casas, who went to America came

[1] Quoted by L. Hanke in *Aristotle and the American Indians* (London: Hollis and Carter; 1959), p. 48.

back, as many missionaries since have done, to report the appalling cruelty of his own countrymen,
so great that he feared God would destroy Spain
for her misdeeds. They were seizing the stored-up
treasures of the Amerindian civilization, mutilating
prisoners, taking the lands, and turning the inhabitants into slaves. Las Casas appealed to the
Spanish sovereigns, Ferdinand and Isabella, for
justice. There followed a deeply interesting debate.
Another cleric opposed him and this man appealed
to Aristotle, who had considered this issue, as indeed he had considered most others. Although Aristotle was not always consistent about this, he
did lay down that the art of war could be practised
against men who, "though intended by nature to
be governed, will not submit, for war of this kind
is naturally just." In another passage he rubbed
the basic point home: "Some men are by nature
free and others slaves, and for these latter slavery
is both expedient and just." "By nature"—here
are the key words, with the injurious idea to be so
often repeated or implied.

In opposition to his opponents' plea that by
Spanish standards the Amerindians were hardly
human, Las Casas made the noble, and as we
now think, the only reply: "All the people of the
world are men." He urged that savage peoples had

been hidden away and forgotten. They were like an "uncultivated soil" bringing forth weeds but with such "natural virtue" that by cultivation it would yield beneficial fruits.[2] But alas! Las Casas himself, while he pitied the poor Amerindians who could not stand up to ill treatment and hard labour, encouraged the importation of African Negroes who were so well able to do so.

The English adventurers and their American descendants dealt out very much the same treatment to the Red Indians in North America. Some of these tribes defied both conquest and slavery. "We are not slaves," said the leader of the Seneca tribe of the famous Six Nations in 1768, speaking of the encroaching colonists. "These forests, these lakes and rivers are ours and before we will part with them we will spatter the leaves with their blood or die every man in the attempt." And so there followed that ghastly long-drawn-out struggle which lives on as material for schoolboy romances and also for the ceaseless manufacture of so-called "western" films, purveyed to satisfy the sense of adventure—or is it the suppressed blood lust?—of our urban civilization. President Theodore Roosevelt wrote the Red Indians' epitaph in his book *The Winning of the West*. "The settler

[2] Ibid., p. 112.

and the pioneers," he concluded, "have at bottom had justice on their side: this great continent could not have been kept as nothing but a game preserve for squalid savages." [3] He thought that only a warped, perverse, and silly morality would take the other view. He added that the life of the Indians was only a few degrees less meaningless than that of the wild beasts with whom they held joint ownership. We may, therefore, be grateful to the late Gary Cooper for stripping the romance from this grim story in his last television commentary before his death. This leads us to ask whether there was no middle course which would have been less brutalizing to the pioneers and less destructive to the Indians.

Before we leave the rest of the colonial world to concentrate upon Africa, we must remark a striking contrast between the natives of that continent and those of the other new lands the Europeans opened up. The world hears nothing at the level of international affairs of Red Indians, Maoris, or Australian aborigines. Their voice is never heard at the United Nations. Nor is that of the sixteen million—a very approximate figure—Amerindians of Central and South America, descend-

[3] Theodore Roosevelt: *The Winning of the West* (New York: Charles Scribner's Sons; 1926), Vol. II, p. 56.

ants, some of them, of empires whose magnificent ruins are studied and admired by Europeans. Yet these Amerindians constitute almost half of the total population of Peru, and in some states they form a large but hitherto neglected and impoverished class. Why has so little been heard of them as a political problem or a political force? Is it because, when South and Central America threw off their colonial rulers, the local immigrant Europeans succeeded to power even in regions where, in those days, they were very greatly outnumbered by the natives? Is it because their relatively smaller numbers, in comparison with Africa, are growing proportionately less as ever more immigrants from Europe and elsewhere reach their continent? Is there some racial weakness, physical or social, that makes it easy to push them aside, or down—that same inability to survive which allowed the Spaniards to sweep the Caribs of the islands so easily into extinction and which makes it so difficult today to preserve the last Amerindian groups of British Guiana? One answer is that the Iberian Roman Catholic Latins who went to southern America, though they might repress and exploit, never placed an unbridgeable gulf between themselves and the natives. Now, although the original natives tend to constitute the lowest class, they are not officially distinguished as such. There is, more-over, a mixed intermediate group below the mainly white class. And this last does not draw an un-yielding colour bar in order to protect itself from the social mobility that allows movement up and down between the three groups until they are more easily distinguishable as classes than as races.

Very different has been the record of Africa in relation to European settlement. West Africa was much too inhospitable to tempt our own seven-teenth- and eighteenth-century forefathers to do more than pick up slaves on the coast. Some West Africans, it is said, told a European that they meant to put up a statue, many, oh! many times life-size, to their great protector and deliverer. The European complacently enquired whether the choice would be Wilberforce or Buxton. "No," came the reply, "the mosquito."

The British immigrants, like the Dutch but quite unlike the Spanish and Portuguese, drew a rigid racial line between themselves and the na-tives. They meant to retain their political control and also the purity of their blood. Hence the an-gry humiliation of the awakening Africans when they tried to make the first grades in the new West-ern civilization and found themselves running right into the impassible colour bar.

The Germanic-speaking Europeans—the British, the Germans, the Americans, the Dutch—share a deep bias against intermarriage with the Negro race. It is no good our trying to avoid this granite hard fact. It lies at the very heart of our present problem in Africa. This conscious, or perhaps unconscious, fear of race mixture accounts both for the white man's innermost ring of defence and for his outer ring of political, social, and economic ramparts. It explains many of the news items that we are getting now from South Africa, from the Rhodesias and Kenya, and from Notting Hill, with the news of occasional retaliatory orgies of the raping of white women in the Congo.

The north-western Europeans are not alone in their fear of intermixture and absorption. The Americans of the United States ought to have some understanding of the race problems of South Africa and the Rhodesias. I did not, however, find it easy to get the analogy accepted when I was lecturing in the States. Yet America's problem is small indeed by contrast. If her Negroes are in a majority in some Southern states, they are a small minority within the powerful nation that contains all the states. In southern Africa the Europeans are a very small minority and their black majority is very far from the degree of Western assimilation that is shown by the American Negroes. That the numerical ratio is closely correlated with the degree of racial discrimination is shown in South America. Yet what white groups have more to fear than those in Africa, where the great preponderance of Africans within their states is now increasingly supported by almost a continent of Africans outside them? Even the coloured world should show some understanding of the fact of discrimination, since among both Asians and New World African groups the lighter skin is regarded as superior to the darker and eagerly sought in marriage. And in Africa itself there are bars of race, if not of colour; I have known a half-Hamite recoil from the idea of marrying a Bantu Negress, and Bantu and Nilotic would be unlikely to mate.

British settlers in tropical Africa are subject to the additional fear, whether conscious or subconscious, of being such tiny minorities. I remember that many years ago, when I was waiting in Aden for a ship to take me across the Gulf of Aden to Somaliland, which was then a pretty wild place, I suddenly felt that I simply could not leave the relative civilization of Aden and plunge into that unknown land across the sea. I do not think it was ordinary physical fear; it certainly was not sexual fear. I think it was the fear that myself, this white, English, self-loved, cultivated self, would in some way be lost, overwhelmed, cut off from its base among tens of thousands of other beings, who were not necessarily inferior but were utterly alien and uncomprehending. This nightmare feeling passed and I do not think I have ever felt anything quite like it either in Somaliland or anywhere else. Yet how many settlers and indeed missionaries, especially in lonely places, may not sometimes add this half-conscious dread to all the other, more rational fears.

It is often said that races are divided by a culture bar as well as by a colour bar. But is there not also a class bar? Many Kenya settlers belonged to what we used to call the gentry, if not the aristocracy; and in earlier days they came from a country that still had strong class divisions. They saw the African tribesmen living in their dark little huts, either naked or clad in greasy goat skins. At home these white men had had no social contact with their servants and labourers—how much less would contact seem possible where the barriers of race and of mutual incomprehension were added to that of status! Communication of any kind would seem impossible at first, except for the giving of half-understood orders.

There was unlimited scope for misunderstanding. I remember the exasperation of a new settler housewife when she found a raw servant from the bush trying to pour water into a kettle through the spout because he did not realize that the lid would come off. But it was a matter for more than exasperation if a new herd-boy fed the milking-herd with poison destined for baboons or other vermin. Worst of all, perhaps, was the threat of disease from straying native cattle or the attention of cattle thieves seeking honours in their own tribe for their exploits. In Southern Rhodesia the settlers, many already toughened by experience in South Africa, had to fight Lobengula's Matabele both in conquest and later in their rebellion. In their view this was a meritorious act because of the bloody tyranny the Matabele had exercised over other tribes. It could not have been easy for the settlers here, or elsewhere in Africa, to adjust their earlier attitudes to the very first educated Africans who arose out of the masses to imitate, or as the settlers might think, to caricature or even to challenge them.

Yet African nationalism today demands its compensation for this long inequality. On their side, the settlers shrink from the idea of living

under African rulers and so the future of the settlers in Kenya and Central Africa hangs in the
balance.

Consider the economic side of the settlers'
case. The regions of the east to which our countrymen migrated differed completely, I must repeat,
from West Africa. The west, for instance, had a
large population. It had many important chiefs
and considerable native states. Its heat and its
soil made its coastal regions something of a natural greenhouse for the steady production of cocoa
and palm oil. And this almost ready-made native
economy meant a ready-made revenue. If Africans
were to be helped to advance, governments must
build up a revenue. For Britain neither could nor
would have poured out the necessary funds at that
time. By contrast with these western regions, Central Africa and Kenya had mostly a poor soil, much
arid steppe, a scanty and ill-distributed rainfall,
and therefore a scanty and ill-distributed population, most of it far more backward in civilization
than that of West Africa. And yet there were some
almost uninhabited areas of high cool land, especially in Kenya, which white settlers might make
richly productive and which might even promise to
repay the early building of a railway.

Settlement could succeed only at the cost of

long, very practical, and scientific experiments in types of soil, of seed, of livestock, and in very hard-bought experience of the fickle climate.[4] In Southern Rhodesia there were minerals—asbestos, gold, chromium, coal—and these set the production graphs climbing up and the industrial development followed. In Northern Rhodesia you can see today a string of mines rearing their shaft-heads out of the virgin bush and belching out their flaming slag. Between 1945 and 1952, to give one example, the output of copper rocketed in value from about £7 million to nearly £70 million per annum. Unlike West Africa, therefore, these countries have now complex, one might say European-type, economies, very dependent upon scientific research, upon capital, and upon managerial skill. Their African populations are increasingly dependent upon earning wages. Settlers, not unnaturally, ask how these new and still precarious economic structures could be put tomorrow under the control of inexperienced African governments.

This is the economic side. On the human side, the settlers, above all the farmers, have committed

[4] The problem of European settlement can be studied, in biographical form, in Elspeth Huxley: *White Man's Country: Lord Delamere and the Making of Kenya* (London: Chatto and Windus; 1935).

themselves, their resources, and their families to Africa. They did not go out as philanthropists, but most of them, after taking one look at Africa, saw themselves—and still see themselves—as the agents of civilization. I think especially of Kenya, of some of my friends who put their small fortunes, perhaps their officers' gratuity, into a raw block of veld. They bashed it into shape, built a small house, and ran in and out of debt as prices or climate failed them. The wife would make a garden with the glorious range of Kenya's flowers, and she would care, as so many have done, for their African labourers, and their labourers' wives and children. It is so much more than an economic problem. These countrymen of ours have given all their hearts and their hopes to that magnificent land. And today they must choose—either to stay under an African government or else to pull out, perhaps impoverished, perhaps in middle or late age, to face a new life, and abandon all they have been struggling to create.

We must turn to look at the African's side. He now sees himself as having been treated as a despised inferior, discriminated against, his social life disrupted by labour migration and by other forces. This in his own country and as the result, as he sees it, of the recent intrusion of white men!

Above all, he fears for his land. It is the land of his family and of his fathers, of their spirits and their graves, and the security for his family and for his own old age. Add to this the political aspect. Here we come to Aristotle again, for it was part of the settlers' earlier case that the Africans were inherently unfit to rule—in fact, "intended by nature to be governed." Here came the argument about the two thousand years which, they said, it had taken Britain to reach her present civilization. In the thirties I sometimes used to study the Nairobi *East African Standard,* in which I would read the settlers' angry speeches and letters, attacking the government and doing so very often for its protection of African interests. The settlers even talked at one time of rebellion. More and more Africans were also reading this newspaper, and I would weigh the cumulative effects on these readers, who were getting, surely, no very good example of civic behaviour. I would hear the not uncommon light remark by settlers, who could have no acquaintance with the dimensions of evolution, that Africans were "just off the trees."

Is it unfair to the settlers to remember these things now, when relations are so different and so difficult? Is it fair to the Africans *not* to remember that this was the atmosphere in which their first bewilderment could harden into the resentment of an almost incurable humiliation? The Africans feared that they would win their struggle to gain what they called "self-government" as they had in South Africa and—a much nearer parallel—in Southern Rhodesia. Actually, about 1930, they very nearly did win, and I well remember the intense struggle in Britain of those of us who opposed that surrender.

But for the African masses the land issue, I think, was always closer and more crucial. Many investigators, and one very thorough commission,[5] have measured the exact amount of inhabited land that was taken from Africans in Kenya. It was, in fact, a very small proportion of the whole. Africans had naturally concentrated upon the best-watered areas and the great bulk of these they retain. But few Africans will accept the figures. This is because their numbers have swelled under Britain's peace and social services and because they now produce more and need more. They look out of their little plots to the large neighbouring European farms. Some of them hold the precarious tenure of squatters on land which, they claim, be-

[5] *Report of the Kenya Land Commission*, Cmd. 4556 (London: H.M.S.O.; 1934).

longs to their tribe. It was the Kikuyu tribe who suffered most from these resentments. Their lovely wooded hills stretch down from the foot of their sacred Mount Kenya to lap almost around Nairobi. They go out to work in large numbers on the European farms. They crowd into the capital and gaze at the European luxuries through the plate-glass windows. They are the most ambitious, the most sophisticated, perhaps the ablest of the Kenya tribes. Their minds became full of bitter anger and envy and they were open therefore to incitement from without.

This brings us to Mau Mau, that most ghastly of rebellions, with its bestial oaths and its cult of torture and murder. Today we busy ourselves studying the psychology of frustration both in nations and in classes and all the perversities into which frustration can drive its victims. A Kenya leader said in effect the other day: "Call us savages and we will go back to savagery." How deep must have been the frustrations of the Kikuyu to drive them to practices that quite deliberately violated the sanctities of their own sexual and tribal life! Both morally and physically the outbreak injured them far more than the settlers. By the end of it, some 80,000 were in detention; how many were killed in the fighting, how many loyalists were murdered, cannot be known. I can never forget the look I saw in the eyes of the so-called hard-core prisoners, both men and women—dark faces made so much darker by their look of settled hate. But I also remember visiting a Christian mission station in the middle of the worst Mau Mau area and seeing the African teachers and clergy go out in the morning on bicycles and motorcycles to carry on with their work in the bush, not knowing whether they would be tortured or murdered or both. Some were killed; others bore the marks of torture, yet their resolution and serenity were un-faltering. The Europeans lost surprisingly few to the Kikuyu knives. My own visits to Kikuyu coun-try during the Mau Mau rebellion were brief, but I was there long enough to know what it was to wonder if a noise in the night meant that *they* were coming. It was a fear much worse than that of any London air-raid, and one which the settlers on their isolated farms, often women alone with their children, had to endure for two or three years on end. And yet—if there had been no white set-tlement, would there have been Mau Mau?

We British, I think, hate to admit that the blackmail of violence can pay. Yet, even before Mau Mau ended, the government made such vig-orous efforts to divert the energies of the disordered

Kikuyu to agriculture that this tribe can now show perhaps the best farming in Africa: it grows some of the best quality coffee and is advancing fast with tea. The government actually began to force the tribe not only to concentrate into villages but also—what is, for Africa, a most revolutionary advance—to accept individual tenure of land. But Mau Mau had even wider political results. This one tribe had disrupted the whole life of the colony, had demanded the mobilisation of all its resources, the dispatch of British troops, and the expenditure of some £60 million. Only one conclusion could be drawn from this, that Kenya could never again face another tribal movement of this kind, still less a movement that encompassed more than a single tribe. That in turn must surely mean that the Kenya Africans could not for long be denied the independence which had been given to the Sudan and to Ghana, which had been promised to backward Somaliland, and which was clearly coming to Tanganyika and Uganda.

Hence the Lancaster House Conference of 1960, when Mr. Macleod courageously—the courage was against a wing of his own party—shattered such illusions as the settlers still cherished about their future. I believe—and this is the belief that has always guided me in the Kenya controversy—

that the situation would be much more serious for both sides today if the settlers had succeeded in gaining their so-called self-government and had entrenched themselves more strongly, yet still hopelessly, in the heart of black tropical Africa.

We must next consider Central Africa. Sir Roy Welensky is a courageous man, but he has his back to the wall and from there he has had some pretty hard things to say about Britain and our erratic conscience. But surely the original mistake was in our ever agreeing to the Central African Federation of 1953. If we had seen Africa steadily, seen it whole, and seen it ahead, we should have realized that this was, to say the least, a highly precarious experiment. Why was it ever attempted?

The Rhodesian settlers, especially those in the all but independent Southern Rhodesia, felt themselves in danger of being caught between two fires —Afrikaner nationalism to the south, African nationalism to the north. British governments on their side saw that, if Southern Rhodesia were to gravitate bit by bit from weakness into the orbit of South Africa, then both *apartheid* and Afrikanerdom would creep north to those territories still under the Colonial Office and would perhaps, in the end, absorb Northern Rhodesia, which already had many Afrikaner miners. It would then come

up sharp against the African nationalism of Nyasaland and of a Tanganyika, which, because it was
a United Nations Trust Territory, was interna-
tionally assured of its independence. But if the two
Rhodesias and Nyasaland, already very much of
an economic unit, could become a political unit, a
large and potentially rich Commonwealth dominion would be born. Southern Rhodesia might then
liberalize further her own native policy; and the
whole region would achieve a more equal system
than *apartheid*, one capable perhaps, under British
influence, of still further liberalization.

That was the case, and it *seemed* reasonable.
But it failed to measure the deeper forces—irra-
tional forces, if you will—against it. Its shock
awoke the still politically somnolent northern Africans. They suddenly realized that the traditional
Colonial Office path that seemed to be leading
slowly forward to self-government was being closed.
Instead, they were being placed under the control
of the Southern Rhodesian settlers. Almost all native races have been quick to recognize the difference between a distant imperial government and
its all too near emigrant subjects. Even the Red
Indians knew the difference, and the attempts of
the British government to protect them from the
lawless advance of the white frontiersmen was one

of the several causes of the American Revolution. The Maoris knew it. So did the famous Chief Khama, father of Tshekedi, who bought a top hat and a frock coat and went to London to protest to Mr. Joseph Chamberlain about the goings-on of Cecil Rhodes—and won his case.

The Africans of Northern Rhodesia and Nyasaland shared this attitude. How could tribes on one side of a frontier be expected to accept settler control while tribes just over the border—tribes they could see, who might even be part of their own group—advanced freely into independence? The political leaders of Nyasaland, that beautiful crowded little land of lakes and mountains, deliberately imported Dr. Banda as their charismatic leader from overseas. Very soon after this they felt driven to prove to us by bloodshed their rejection of the Federation. Even the Southern Rhodesian Africans, who had apparently been docile under the admittedly very intelligent and paternal rule of their settler government, began to feel the stirrings of nationalism. I attended one of the first large political meetings of Africans in the native quarter of the capital, Salisbury. I remember that packed hall and how electric it was with the current of suddenly aroused racial assertion and resolve.

The gap between the races was revealed, and alas! it has widened. Attempts have been made to close it in Southern Rhodesia with relaxations of the colour bar, generous educational and other welfare services, and a new multi-racial university. Some Africans are at last to be admitted even to the Southern Rhodesian parliament. Ingeniously weighted franchises were devised which would favour education and wealth, in order to give the Europeans political predominance now and at the same time allow Africans to qualify increasingly, as they advanced little by little in civilization. On paper, I think we must admit, this gradualism may seem just what was needed for a measured closure of the gap between the races. It seemed to reflect Britain's development of a middle class and her step-by-step extension of political equality to match that of economic and educational standards. But the Africans had by now been infected with more impatient hopes. Their leaders today prefer to be at the head of the African masses, to urge them on to total victory, rather than to be the camp-followers, tagging along in the rear of the white man's forces. The width of the racial divide is shown by the tragic fall of nearly all, whether white or black, who have tried honestly to reach across from one side to the other as intermediaries.

Both sides tend to regard them as traitors or "stooges," though they may in fact be suffering for their courage and liberalism. Africans especially deal out relentless intimidation to their own small minority of moderate and experienced Africans who try to stand against the extremist current. That same intimidation, we may note, is wielded in other racial situations—by white men in America's black South and even more terribly today by both colonist and native in Algeria.

The future of these settled areas is at present open to many questions. In Central Africa, will the local Europeans be able to retain control long enough to impose *their* standards of civilization, *their* pace of advance, and also persuade Britain to agree? Will the Africans, especially the workers in the mines and industries, realize their own economic interest in retaining the Federation, and with it European control of a complex economy which surely they cannot for many years hope to manage efficiently themselves? In Kenya, the main political issue is now settled. The responsibility of power might incline an African government to safeguard the productive settlers, who are estimated to provide some 90 per cent of the agricultural exports. Unfortunately, the scattered and heterogeneous tribes would have made unity difficult even if there had been no settlers, no Asians, no Arab coast, no irredentist Somalis in the north. Should the new African government use violent measures to coerce dissidents, should there be a break-down of security, very few Europeans would wish to live under these conditions. The bitterness of the settlers at being treated, as they see it, by Britain, their own country, as expendable is beyond measure. Compensation for them would present political and administrative problems, and yet surely the nation whose governments encouraged them to settle, and to believe even to the eleventh hour that their position would be protected, owes them compensation?

There are times when it seems that the problems Africa sets to black alone, and certainly to black and white living together, are beyond a rational solution. It is not easy for white men, above all those whose lives are committed to Africa, even to plan a just course between the kind of freedom exhibited in the Congo and the kind of order exhibited in South Africa. All the more since, though man does not live by bread alone, he does need the bread that only a stable economy can provide in this physically poor and precarious continent. Yet the Africans can no longer be ruled as if they were merely ciphers without names or minds. In most of Africa they are taking over their own destiny, taking it into inexperienced, fumbling, and sometimes violent, yet eager and vigorous hands. Where power has been given, it cannot now be taken back from the Africans, certainly not by their former rulers. Whether it can long be denied by those white minorities that still so desperately retain it will probably be settled in the next two or three years. But the present omens seem to point to the removal from Africa, after their brief presence, of both European rule and European colonization and the reversion of the whole continent to the control of its black and brown inhabitants.

V

The Colonial Account

THE TITLE of this lecture should not arouse the expectation that I am going to draw up an imperial balance sheet with all Britain's beneficent acts upon one side and all her errors on the other, and then see if we end up with a moral credit or a debit. I can do no more than look back over our record, again mainly in Africa, suggest some of the criteria for judgement, and offer some very personal opinions.

To attempt to judge an empire would be somewhat like approaching an elephant with a tape-measure. The size and the shape of the object baffles us; moreover, being alive, it will not keep still. And what criteria should we use—whether the empire benefited the ruler or the ruled? The question sounds absurd today because it is now taken completely for granted that the only test is the interests of the ruled. Yet this is a new test. It would be wholly misleading to apply it to the entire record of the British Empire, which, like all other empires, was created and conducted mainly in the interests of the ruling power. The structure and the policies of the Empire were moulded at a time when this idea predominated, and much remoulding has had to be done to adjust the Empire to a new age. To understand the imperial terminus we must therefore look back, however briefly, over the course, in order to see what Britain at different times thought was the main purpose of empire.

Looking back over that record, we can identify five main purposes which led Britain to build an empire. They were neither all simultaneous nor all neatly consecutive. There was the economic purpose, mainly the expansion of trade. This itself created the further purpose of security, the need to protect our world-wide commerce, an ever increasing need. Lord Salisbury once said that he feared the military would advise him to garrison the moon to protect us from Mars—not quite such a fantastic witticism now as it was in his day. Emigration proved another purpose; and these three aims of empire were embodied in the latter part of the nineteenth century and the earlier part of the twentieth in what then came to be regarded as the supreme purpose of empire, the attainment and enjoyment of power and prestige. From the eighteenth century, however, there slowly grew a fifth and fairly constant purpose, the challenging ideal of philanthropy, and this alone saw the interests of the ruled as equal, if not indeed superior, to those of the rulers.

Let us consider some of these purposes. Our first period of empire—this is, of course, the shorthand of history—was dominated by the mercantile concept. The aim was to obtain a favourable balance of trade by importing raw materials and exporting English manufactures in English ships. Colonies were very useful parts of the system: they could produce at least some of the needed raw materials, and they could be prevented from competing with manufactures, for the interests of the colonies, as indeed of Ireland, were regarded as wholly subservient to those of Britain. The original Elizabethan concept of colonialism had been very simple. Sir Francis Drake, in commending colonial expansion to his countrymen, in very bad verse, remarked of the American Indians:

Their gain shall be the knowledge of our faith,
And ours such riches as the country hath.

It was during this well-known, long-enduring mercantile period that the greatest single and most obvious crime of imperialism was committed—that of the African slave trade, by which Africa, and especially West Africa, was drained of its man power to provide labour for the plantations of the Americas and the Caribbean. It is no mitigation of the guilt that, as slavery existed in Africa, the slave merchants did not have to go slave-hunting themselves but were conveniently provided with their goods at the coast by African intermediaries. Of course the ready market for slaves stimulated tribal wars and forays in the interior. The world has seen slavery in many forms, but this was perhaps the worst kind of slavery the world had known. It took the slaves to a different continent, where they were so strikingly distinct in form and colour from the free population that their slave status and, after freedom, their still inferior status as ex-slaves, was always visible, with results that are very much with us today. Africans seem more interested now in recent than in ancient wrongs. But in this matter of slavery, in view of the unimaginable sufferings it caused millions of their forefathers and the solid benefits our own derived from it, the Africans, and still more the West Indians, have a long-antedated cheque in hand which we ought to try to honour.

Here, then, in our colonial reckoning, whatever else is uncertain, we can write on the debit side one unalleviated, unquestionable, widespread, long-continuing, and highly profitable crime.

As the eighteenth century moved into its third quarter, the British conscience was increasingly aroused against the abuses of empire, above all against the slave trade. The attack came from several quarters. To the Christians, first the Quakers and then the new Christian evangelical movement, slavery was sin. To the new romantic movement it was ugly. To the new radical philosophers it was unnatural. To the new liberal economists it was uneconomic. The streams converged, but the religious impulse, which was directed politically by Wilberforce, Buxton, and many others, provided the strongest and most constant pressure towards the abolition, first of the trade and then, in 1833, of the institution of slavery—some thirty

years, it is interesting to note, before the abolition of serfdom in Russia.

The effect of the anti-slavery movement went
far deeper than the abolition. The long and inten-
sive propaganda throughout the country—even
children were persuaded not to eat sweets made
with slave-grown sugar—bit deeply into the nation's thinking. The lesson was that once out of
sight of Britain the white man could not be
trusted to deal justly with the black man. The
price of humanity abroad was therefore eternal vigi-
lance at home. The abolitionists went on to obtain a
parliamentary committee, which reported in the
most altruistic and idealistic terms ever achieved,
perhaps, in any parliamentary document.[1] God, it
said, would require of Britain an accounting of
how she had used her power over "untutored and
defenceless savages." Again: "Our system has in-
curred a vast load of crime." [2] The committee was
not content with generalizations. It took a mass
of evidence. For the first time an African was
called to Westminster to testify on behalf of his
people. A detailed description of the sins of em-

[1] *Report from the Select Committee on Aborigines,* 1837, VII,
425 (reprinted by the Aborigines Protection Society, London,
1837).
[2] Ibid., pp. 105-6.

pire was presented—territory usurped, European vices and diseases introduced, brandy and gunpowder disseminated. Examples were given of the treatment of natives in North and South America, the West Indies, New Zealand, the Pacific Islands, and Australia. But about half the report was concerned with South Africa, where missionaries had been active in making protests and in supplying information. The main conclusion was certainly unique for any official document. "The British Empire has been signally blessed by Providence in her eminence, her strength, her wealth, her prosperity. . . . These were given for some higher purpose than commercial prosperity and military renown. . . . He who has made Great Britain what she is will require at our hands how we have employed the influence He has lent to us in our dealings with the untutored and defenceless savages." [3]

Here, then, was a new standard by which to judge the Empire. By the seventeenth- and eighteenth-century standards of the mercantilists our empire, and especially the slave trade that it made possible, was a resounding success. By the standard of "the Saints," as the humanitarian leaders were sometimes called, our imperial activities were very largely sinful. The interests of the natives—

[3] Ibid., p. 105.

here, indeed, was a new and revolutionary standard—should actually be put before our own. The
altruism of this report should level up to the demands of the modern anti-colonialists, though they
might not relish the purely religious principles by
which the demands were supported. The humanitarians could not, as it turned out, maintain their
temporary ascendancy. Yet the standard they left
has never been wholly lost. It became part of Britain's public life, maintained by individuals of all
parties or of none, and especially by the churches,
and the tradition has acted as a strong palliative,
if not a cure, for the evils to which empire was
prone.

The abolitionists, being very practical men, ensured that the public challenge of their standard
should be maintained by founding a society—or
rather two linked societies, the Anti-Slavery and
the Aborigines Protection societies, which were
combined in 1909. Ever since their day, therefore,
there has been an organization in London, spon-
sored by members of Parliament and leading philanthropists, which has collected and communi-
cated information about abuses from all over the
Empire, and also from foreign sources. This organization has led deputations to the Colonial or
Foreign Secretary and has provided M.P.'s with

material out of which to frame awkward parliamentary questions or to initiate debates.

I once had a personal experience of the effectiveness of the Society's work. I was staying with a governor in an African territory about which the Society had raised a parliamentary question concerning the methods used to recruit labour for work on a new railway. The governor was complaining about this intervention and I felt obliged to confess that I was at that time on the Society's executive committee. Without a word the governor rose from the table—we were at dinner—and went to his office. He came back staggering under a load of files. *"This,"* he said, "is what you and your friends have inflicted upon a busy governor who had better things to do!" I forget now how far the accusations were justified. But even if they had not been, I would still feel that, on balance, the Society has acted as a continuous and beneficial restraint.

The dominance of the philanthropists was soon challenged. The emigration motive came to the fore. This has always been, as we saw in my last talk, by its very nature the greatest challenge to philanthropic and Christian attempts to protect native rights. As soon as colonists began to occupy lands that the natives claimed and these retaliated, often in brutal fashion, the philanthropists and the defenders of the colonists met in passionate conflict in Britain. This has been a continuing theme of our colonial history from our first contacts with the Red Indians until today, when the issues are in East and Central Africa. The conflict of policies exists, of course, not only in Britain. The emigrants can set up new centres of power and policy-making which, as we saw in the last lecture, can challenge the control, often the more humane and just control, of the metropolitan power. So the theme of disputed power runs beside that of disputed morality, and we can trace this conflict also, certainly from Roman days, to the tragic current events in Algeria and, again, to those facing Britain in East and Central Africa.

In the mid-nineteenth century the economic motive for empire went dramatically into reverse over its methods. Britain swung around from believing that colonial possessions were necessary to her trade to the exactly opposite belief that they were an unnecessary embarrassment and expense. This, of course, was because her great lead in the industrial revolution gave her an unchallengeable export market. In this state of mind she was so ready to relax her control of the older settled

colonies that, paradoxically, she won their un-
forced loyalty and so laid the foundations of the
Commonwealth. She was also setting a precedent
in political emancipation which other than white
subjects would later claim. It is interesting to remember that in some instances she even refused
annexation requested by native peoples. The case
of the Cameroons is an example. What an even
greater state Nigeria would be today if its territory
rounded the Gulf of Guinea! In the sixties the possibility was seriously considered of abandoning all
the West African possessions except Sierra Leone.
Again we may ask whether Ghana would have pro-
gressed to her present level of wealth and education if the Gold Coast had been left, like Liberia,
in the poverty and semi-isolation of independence.

By the end of the nineteenth century economic
interest had swung round again to regard imperial power as an economic necessity. Other nations
had acquired Britain's industrial magic and also
her former imperial ambitions. Great wars were
waged once more in Europe; large armies were
raised; fragmented countries were unified. Britain
had to look to her security. Her new commercial
competitors, moreover, did not follow her free-
trade policy. She was, therefore, afraid of being

shut out of many regions where her traders and missionaries had long been quietly at work. Her missionaries had always been doubtful whether imperial annexation should follow their moral conquests or whether they should run their own little independent theocracies in the wilds. But the horrors of the Arab slave trade, which Livingstone had first revealed eating its way year by year into the healthy flesh of Africa, made them change their minds. So did the fear of French, German, or Portuguese annexation. As a result, philanthropy tended to swing around in support of annexation.

By the end of the century, therefore, we find Britain reacting vigorously to *all* the motives for empire: trade, security, emigration, philanthropy, all converging to produce the crowning motive, the enjoyment of power and prestige, dramatically visible on the world map with its generous distribution of the colour red.

Many writers have described this strange and, as I think, uncharacteristic outburst. There was the military element in it illustrated by the famous couplet:

We don't want to fight, but by jingo, if we do
We've got the men, we've got the ships, we've
got the money too.

There was the myth of a superior race fostered by the application of Darwinian ideas of the survival of the fittest to human history. There was in some quarters a renewal of that assumption of a divine-mission which had supported some of the earliest of the world's emperors, a mission to bring order and civilization to lower races. Lord Curzon said that "the British Empire was, under Providence, the greatest instrument for good that the world has seen." Lord Rosebery saw in our success "the finger of the Divine." And there was high confidence. "The future," said Chamberlain, "is with the great Empires and there is no greater Empire than the British." That strange genius Kipling had by his stories and verses made the Empire, and above all India, real, very human, and dramatic to the man in the street and the boy in the school. But for a moment even he, as he contemplated our dominion over palm and pine in 1897, was almost afraid before his God, that Britain might become "drunk with sight of power." Nor was the old mercantile spirit dead. There were times when men forgot the generally low estimate of Africa's possibilities, and its tropical regions were seen as a great potential producer of raw materials which should feed the machines of our factories and so, indirectly, the mouths of our growing industrial masses. And Chamberlain, for one, did not see how this could be done if we clung to our principle of free trade.[4]

It was a heady moment. Yet Britain did not altogether lose her head. There were at least three correctives to this state of exaltation. One was that a very large part of the Empire consisted of the all but self-governing settled colonies and Britain accepted and even gloried in their freedom, though many people in Britain wanted to strengthen the Empire by weaving a closer, even a federal, tie with them. But these new nations were developing clear wills of their own, especially with regard to their own economic interests. They resisted ideas of imperial federation and their stubborn nationalism, especially that of Canada, was a hard reminder to Britain of the limits of her influence. The second corrective was that even the more politically famous lyricists of empire were not always living at such heights of euphoria. Their verbal extremes should be weighed against a large volume of practical humane utterance and, more important, of work accomplished in this spirit. And third, in order to counteract the extravagances

[4] For a general account of British imperial thought at this period, see William L. Langer: *The Diplomacy of Imperialism* (New York: Alfred A. Knopf; 1951). Sections II & III.

of imperialism, there was a great weight in Parliament and outside not only of humanitarian but also of critical liberal opinion. Further, to puncture the balloon of British self-esteem and let out the gas, there were critics, irreverent men like Bernard Shaw and H. G. Wells, who wrote so well that they simply *had* to be read.

The new century was not very old, moreover, before a jarring note was struck. Britain's coloured subjects began, first in India, to assert *their* criterion of empire, that it should extend the precedent set by the white dominions and lead *all* its peoples to greater self-government—the word *independence* was hardly used as yet.

There thus began a period of divided views about the ultimate purpose of empire. For Britain did not at first accept the opinion of her coloured subjects. She did not flatly reject the application of the new criterion to her colonies; but as regards those in Africa at least, her references to self-government in the first two or three decades of this century were couched in vague and rather distant terms.

One reason for this attitude lay in the serious doubts, held in the earlier years of this century, whether Eastern and African races were capable of parliamentary government, or a slightly different point, whether it was suitable for them. This doubt arose partly, no doubt, from the deep, unexpressed distaste for the idea of abdicating authority —and how many nations have ever willingly given up power? Some of the prominent men who voiced these doubts, Milner, Cromer, Lugard, Curzon, spoke out of the confidence that comes from what may be man's most intoxicating experience—the wielding of great personal authority. Yet they were right in thinking that for peoples who had not invented parliamentary democracy and had resorted all through history to altogether other methods of rule the sudden adoption of this Western system might be too revolutionary a step. Moreover, had not the ruler of millions some reason for hesitating to hand over his authority to the first score or hundred of self-appointed applicants who asked for it? When, for instance, the intelligentsia of Lagos asked Lugard to recognize them as the leaders and spokesmen of Nigeria, he could answer truly enough that most of them had never been more than a few dozen miles inland and that nearly all the hundred or so rulers of the vast hinterland had never so much as heard of them.

Africans, following Asians, pressed on, as we saw, ignoring the doubts or negations of their rulers. In Africa the period between the moment, in any territory, when independence with democracy became a possibility and the moment when it was achieved was brief indeed. Yet the Africans think it was too long, and as this is one of their main complaints we must ask whether it could have been even shorter if we had had more foresight. It may be that only autocratic governments attempt to foresee—and then they often see the wrong things. I think that many of us who were involved in colonial affairs between the wars were taken by surprise by the speed with which African nationalism advanced. But much of the official world seemed even more myopic. I remember, at the end of a conference on West Africa in 1939, a senior man from the Colonial Office concluding his talk with the remark: "Well, at any rate in Africa we can be sure that we have unlimited time in which to work."

Perhaps the reason for this degree of blindness is that British people do not understand nationalism, do not recognize it, or at least its strength, in others. Our exceptional unity, our island position, and the confidence arising from our former power may have bred in us an unconscious kind of nationalism, one that seldom needed to assert or even know itself. Looking back, I must admit my own slowness in realizing why, in spite of all the advantages colonial rule had, as it seemed to me, so manifestly brought to them, educated Africans still seemed bitterly discontented.

I think that we made a serious miscalculation about our power to control the pace of political advance in our colonies. Most of us concerned with colonial affairs erred in some degree. We had two motives for attempting delay. One was the deep unspoken reluctance, to which I have just alluded, to resign imperial power and all the advantages that seemed to go with it. The other—and who can measure even in one person the exact proportion of these two motives?—was the belief, the well-founded belief, in my view, that the African peoples needed a further period of colonial rule before independence with democracy could be given a really propitious start. Even so, and in spite of much that we achieved in the thirties and forties, we should surely have been even more urgent, especially after the Second World War, in working for both the unity and the kind of education which self-government would demand.

One reason for our difficulty in pressing the many necessary adjustments may have been that we were so deeply committed to indirect rule. Our critics, of course, like to ascribe our attitude to a deep-laid scheme to prolong our power by crystallising tribalism, for, as long as a dependency's political and administrative life was in parts, the colonial power must continue to maintain the whole. There is much truth in this charge. But we also had more generous and more scientific motives. In the thirties I sat at the feet of Professor Malinowski, alongside some brilliant young anthropologists, who went on to bury themselves for a year or two within a single African tribe, learning its language and customs and emerging finally to report what a wonderfully integrated but brittle social mechanism they had been observing. It would surely, so we then thought, be ruthless and arrogant roughly to impose upon these societies our own culture, our own forms of government. The African parts must be helped to grow slowly and naturally, outwards from within, into the larger whole.

There was another, surely not altogether unworthy, motive for resisting too abrupt a departure from indirect rule. Many Africans today write off chiefs as if they were stooges. But hereditary chiefs had great power or influence when Africa was first annexed. They took the strain of indirect rule, breaking down, like human transformers, the powerful current from above and distributing it in voltages that their own people could take. Officials who had learned to trust them naturally hesitated, as times changed, to throw over men who had been their loyal and often able co-workers, sometimes their friends. Imperial power tends to lean for support upon such groups as have local power at a given moment and in Africa that has meant both chiefs and white settlers. But as time and change weaken these supports, the external power shifts its weight almost automatically to some new solidity. Our history is strewn with the wrecks of such abandoned supports. Among the most impressive of these ruins are the princely states of India. For governments, unlike individuals, are not free to support lost causes. It may look noble to put a king upon an ace, but it does not take the trick.

It should surely have been possible for us, however, to anticipate the coming need for unity and force the pace in that direction. In Northern Nigeria, for instance, I fear that some of our officials became at least as northern as the northerners, fostering the local sense of difference, even of superiority, towards the south. They found it easier to get along with the Moslem northerners on the basis of admitted difference and mutual respect. The relationship with the southerners, who would be at some stage between their old pagan culture and the culture of the West, was often uncertain, even though at best it might be closer than the officials' relationship with the Moslems. The same situation had existed in India between the Hindu and the Moslem. In the Sudan we accepted, we almost intensified, the division between Arab north and pagan south, doing all too little to foster a mutual understanding before we went away and left them together in a perilous association. The clash that followed may have been unavoidable, but it might not have been so tragic if we had fostered more mutual understanding. In Nyasaland and in Northern Rhodesia, was it wise almost at the eleventh hour to try to set chiefs in the forefront of the battle against nationalists, since nationalists, after all, had the future in their hands?

Self-government would demand not only unity but hundreds of men and women trained for the technical and other services of a modern state. In East and Central Africa, above all, this essential élite hardly exists, and politics absorb all too many of the few educated men. It has even been said that here Africans can rule but do little else, since the necessary experts all have to be imported. Even in Nigeria, especially Northern Nigeria, the need is great. Professor Harbison, the American who assisted the education commission headed by Sir

Eric Ashby, said in the report that ideally Nigeria needed 80,000 graduates in the next ten years.[5] Of course I am not suggesting that nothing was done. The education adviser at the Colonial Office and his staff worked and travelled tirelessly to stimulate and co-ordinate the departments in the colonies. But in nearly all African dependencies resources were never enough to meet the pressing demands for advance in every direction. Yet there was nothing the African taxpayer cared about more than he cared about education; the immediately increased funds and efforts put into education, at the expense of all other services, as Africans attained independence, show that for them this was the first of all demands. It must be remembered, however, that in the earlier decades of this century Africans in many if not most regions were indifferent or suspicious about Western education. Often there was real hostility. This was especially true of female education, and today one of the tragedies of Africa is the great gap in understanding between educated men and their womenfolk, often even between political leaders and their wives. Higher education could be built only upon secondary education, and

[5] *Investment in Education*. The Report of the Commission on Post-School Certificate and Higher Education in Nigeria (Lagos: Federal Press; 1960), p. 7.

so on, it was thought, down the broadening steps
of the pyramid. It was only the later urgency of
the demand for men of higher education to staff
the new states which led to the realization that a
steeple or even a tower would have been a better
simile for an education system than a pyramid. As
it was, since the Second World War nine universities were fostered in Africa by an unofficial Inter-
University Council, which devoted some £16 million of the British taxpayers' money toward the
buildings and other capital expenses. As a member
of the executive committee of this body, I often
marvelled at the energy with which some of the
heads of our own universities, already overworked
in their own posts, laboured in Britain and flew
about Africa and beyond in pursuit of this exciting
but exacting new task. Some of them, as a result,
seriously undermined their health.[6] Nothing we
could do in the time we had and in the face of existing conditions in Africa could ever have been
enough. But some of the governments should have
fulfilled the main purpose of all this education,
even in the last few years of their rule, by an urgent, even a "crash," program of training and promotion. This would have given more young Afri-

[6] For a brief account of this work see Alexander Carr-Saunders:
New Universities Overseas (London: Allen & Unwin; 1961).

cans the experience and confidence needed to assume the task of administration when the politicians took over the government.

No attempt to reckon up the uses and abuses of Britain's colonial rule would be complete if it did not try to evaluate the agency through which this rule was carried out—the Colonial Office and the Colonial Service. Consider how the colonial chain of command ran from Britain to the African colonies. It begins with a largely ignorant public as the ultimate source of policy; an overloaded Parliament; a Colonial Office for which decentralization was a principle, indeed a necessity; the sundering ocean. And on the other side, in the colonies themselves, there were the governors and their staffs, with great powers to use or abuse.

Much could be said of each of these links, but I must confine myself to a brief treatment of the Colonial Office, giving somewhat more attention to the Colonial Service.

The Colonial Office has a long and fascinating history, but here only the most recent years can be touched upon. Its largest task in this century was in Africa and its structure was constantly being adjusted, especially after the work for the Dominions was placed under a separate department in 1925. Its tasks grew as the widening conception of the scope of government was reflected in Africa. When Britain is criticized for not having begun this or that social service in Africa at some early date, it is often forgotten that in Britain herself such functions were only gradually regarded as proper to the state.

From dealing with the colonies largely through geographical departments, and largely in regard to administration in a restricted sense, the Office burgeoned out into a number of new departments, dealing generally with the whole Empire and concerned with economics, social services, information, students, and other matters. The Office forged links between itself and the colonies and between these and expert opinion in Britain by an increase in the number of its specialist advisers and advisory committees. These were widely representative of the best available knowledge in the country. The process had begun before the period and continued to expand almost until today. By the middle fifties there were twenty-five advisers. Most of them were constantly on tour, stimulating the departments overseas and returning to headquarters with news and views. By that same period there were twenty-eight advisory committees concerned with the principal services rendered to the colonies. Their chief fault was that they poured out too many ideas of reform and advancement for a busy Office to convert into policy and execute. I sat for some years on the education advisory committee and have seldom worked in a more enthusiastic and businesslike body. It acted, with the relevant Office staff and the advisers, as a dynamic link between the educational world of this country and the education departments overseas. Not least, it educated the educators of this country about the colonies.

The Office had, of course, its defects. Most of these were inherent in its position. It tended, in the exact sense of the word, to be irresponsible because it could not be made answerable to any public opinion. That of Britain was almost inevitably too ignorant and ill-informed; and until recent years that of the colonial peoples had no effective existence. Fortunately, early in the nineteenth century, largely through the influence of a great permanent under-secretary, Sir James Stephen, himself one of the humanitarians, the Office was endowed with a tradition of trusteeship, and so with a bias that its staff showed whenever they were free to do so in the interests of the colonial peoples.

To the inevitable irresponsibility of the Office must be added the difficulty of finding general principles that could apply to *all* the various and numerous dependencies. Moreover, secretaries of state for the colonies were frequently changed and few of them, with notable exceptions, had the time or the capacity to achieve a mental mastery over their vast responsibilities. In so far as British governments failed to give clear political directives in their colonial policies, and failed to foresee the trend of events, these were some of the underlying reasons.

One other defect may be mentioned. The Colonial Service grew in numbers and the Office developed an increasing control over it. This was a large task. A colonial governor once complained to me that the Office was so busy administering the Colonial Service that it had no time to administer the colonial empire. It was not, of course, its task to *administer* the colonies: that indeed was the business of the governors, acting under general instructions. But it is possible that too much attention was paid to the interests of the officials, especially the governors. One result was a tendency to send the best men and the best staff to the more important colonies and to apply the reverse policy to the smaller and poorer colonies. From my experience of some of the colonies, especially in earlier days, I would say that too little was done to counter the natural tendency to stagnate. Vigorous governors, with instructions to reform, should have been sent irrespective of questions of pay and precedence.

The trouble was, of course, mainly one of money. Colonies were regarded as separate units both as to administration and as to finance. The idea that colonies should be financed and developed by the British taxpayer was, apart from exceptional circumstances, very late in appearing. Britain had, after all, some forty dependencies and most of them could have pleaded financial need. And Britain was not immune to the effects of depressions herself. Moreover, she was still under the last vestiges of the influence of Draconian, or shall we say Gladstonian, principles of finance, which she extended from the domestic to the imperial sphere. It was held that colonies, like mediaeval kings, should "live of their own," and that this rule was healthier for them, as well as more economical for the metropolis. It was Gladstone's successor as colonial secretary in the forties, Earl Grey, who said: "The surest test for the soundness of measures for the improvement of an uncivilized people is that they should be self-sufficing." In these days of aid with a capital A, such ideas may deserve much of the condemnation that is applied

to them. Yet some economic experts today are beginning to doubt whether the extreme opposite of
this doctrine, the lavish, uncontrolled injection of
capital, may not have its own pathological effects
upon a young economy. From the first, of course,
some grants were given, necessarily, and some
loans were made. But if, after what was regarded as
a fair start, a dependency ran into the red, it was
treated—and here indeed was a fault—not to generous help to get its economy on to a new footing,
but to minimum grants coupled with a severe form
of treasury control. The first hesitant step of the
long progression away from this negative financial
policy, which certainly delayed the advance of
many of the poorer colonies, was the establish-
ment of a modest Colonial Development Fund in
1929. It is a far cry from the million pounds a year
voted then to the £180 million a year paid out in
1961 in all forms of aid and, indeed, to the immense variety of other forms of assistance supplied
by Britain through the new Department of Technical Aid.[7]

---

[7] A summary of the Department's activities will be found in its
first official report, *Technical Assistance from the United Kingdom for Overseas Developments*. Miscellaneous No. 1 Cmd.
(London: H.M.S.O.; 1961).

The Colonial Office was staffed like any other government department in Whitehall. The Colonial Service, though in later years a marginal and temporary interchangeability was introduced, was separate and of course an immensely larger service. Until the later years of the colonial empire the élite of this corps was the Administrative Service.

What sort of men were these last? In his book *The Guardians* Philip Woodruff has given us a brilliant account of the Indian civil service.[8] Much of what he says would apply to the Colonial Administrative Service at its height. Its presiding genius for some thirty years, Sir Ralph Furse, shared Plato's conception of "the Guardians," men nurtured to serve the state and their fellows, just, detached, uncorruptible. In Africa they needed to be all this. There were wide varieties in the physical and human conditions in the colonies. Even within one Northern Nigerian district, for instance, there might be the headquarters of a highly organized Moslem state, which needed little more than expert supervision, and not many miles away there might also be primitive pagans who would shoot poisoned arrows at the young officer who climbed up their rocky

[8] Philip Woodruff: *The Men Who Ruled India* (London: Jonathan Cape; 1954), Vol. II.

fastness to try to persuade them to stop raiding caravans. In 1930 a weighty commission[9] listed the following as desirable qualities for the Administrative Service:

> Vision, high ideals of service, fearless devotion to duty born of a sense of responsibility, tolerance and, above all, team spirit.

Courage and physical prowess might have been added. Where were these qualities to be found? In the public schools and in Oxford and Cambridge. So, at least, the commission believed, and it acted upon its belief.

I can very well imagine some of the repercussions to what I have just said. For there is a fashionable reaction today against the type of man I have mentioned and the tie that he wears. It seems that, to find the impetus to spring from one phase in his development to the next, man often finds it necessary to stamp very heavily upon the phase he is leaving. A Dutch student of British society once argued that the British aristocracy, when faced with the ending of their ascendancy, invented the

[9] *Committee on the System of Appointment in the Colonial Service,* Cmd. 3554 (London: H.M.S.O.; 1930), p. 23.

public schools in order to tame the on-coming bourgeoisie with their traditions of the gentleman. Perhaps for the fallible race of man they might have done worse.

I believe that, in view of its special task in the period, the Colonial Service achieved as much as could have been expected of any large body of men. More, the office of district commissioner should stand out in history as one of the supreme types developed by Britain to meet a special demand, like the office of justice of the peace in Tudor times. The D. C. was for years in almost unqualified control of his district, the would-be father of his people, the jack of all trades, a unit in a service of reliable and interchangeable parts which were by no means robots. He could be relied upon to be humane, uncorrupt, diligent—even when left alone and quite unsupervised in the outer regions of a very testing continent.

I am prepared to admit, looking back, that the Service did gain greatly from some able men who were *not* of the then generally accepted type, outsiders, indeed, who introduced new ideas and methods. Among the dead—for obviously I must not name the living—are Lord Lugard, Sir Donald Cameron, and Sir Gordon Guggisberg; and there were many brilliant and original men of less than gubernatorial rank. But surely a service entirely staffed by geniuses would be unworkable.

As I mentioned in my first lecture, I helped with the courses that were developed for the Service at Oxford, and especially for men—by no means all from Africa—coming back for advanced studies after some years of service in the colonies.

I would meet them again while travelling in Africa. I think my most striking impression of these tours was that the great majority of the men I knew revelled in their work. They generally loved their district and were nearly always eager to point out the virtues rather than the faults of the people under their charge. Indeed, an officer's devotion to his people would often come to be regarded as an official fault by the secretariat, against whom he might champion their causes too intemperately. Paternalism carried too far could become almost a moral fault. Some of the officers, often but not always the young unmarried men, worked immensely long hours with little or no weekend rest. There was need for this, especially in the early thirties, when staff, both administrative and technical, was scanty. A man might have a district the size of a large or medium English county, and its population might number anywhere from twenty thousand to nearly half a million, though in this case he would have one or two assistants, and perhaps a sub-district.

The people seemed to need everything he could do for them, and more. It was certainly a man's job. It could take all he had to give, with every faculty employed at full stretch. And in earlier days it had its discomforts, even its dangers. The official was living in a strange continent that was physically and sometimes humanly violent. My sister, who was married to an administrative officer, was once cut off up the Juba River by a rising of Somalis who murdered the assistant district officer. Another time she woke up one night to find a man about to spear her husband. On another occasion she had to walk and wade for a hundred miles through flooded land in southern Tanganyika, picking the leeches off her legs at frequent intervals. One D.C. friend of mine was killed by an elephant as he stood at the door of his office. Another man I know was killed while hunting a man-eating lion that was terrifying a village. I went once to a very remote district in Tanganyika, and found my host, an assistant district commissioner, in a glorified mud hut. I thought he looked rather strange and

made a preliminary polite enquiry. The reply was
that he would be quite happy if it were not for the
crowds of people from Dar-es-Salaam crowding in
upon him. I discovered that the local people had
decided that the monster crocodile which was taking their children and stock at the river was really
their district officer in another form. Terrified, they
all avoided him. He was the only man not in on
the local secret.

Much of what I have just been saying refers to
the twenties and thirties rather than to later times.
In the following years there was progress in every
way in the conditions of the Service. The number
of white officials at province and district headquarters increased. Measures were devised to break
down the isolation of the Colonial Service and
keep the minds of its men open to new ideas and to
comparative experience. More and more technical
officers were recruited. The district commissioner
was no longer isolated in command: he was the
captain of a team, playing his part in a settled, co-
ordinated plan drawn up for the whole territory,
and playing it in increasing partnership with African councillors and staff.

One fault of the administrator was a tendency
to look down on his technical colleagues. He might

have an overly strong sense of hierarchy, and his unoccupied wife might have even more. But, if the Colonial Service was not a task for the genius, the marvel is that it attracted so many men of high standards of character and education. I have not forgotten the letter I had from one of the first Africans to become an assistant district commissioner, who was posted to some remote sub-station. "I marvel," he wrote, "that an English graduate can endure to live alone in such a place for £400 a year."

The defects of the Service were due less to the faults of its members than to the lack of direction given to it by its masters, all the way from the governors to the British public. A service can respond to a lead and can sustain a tradition, but it cannot create policy. The colonial officials might maintain a reasonably efficient and benevolent administration, but only when their activities were fused into a dominant and stimulating purpose by a good, still more, by a great governor could it give of its best. With regard to the side turned towards the Africans, the Service nearly always numbered too few in relation to the Africans, and it was perhaps too British, to cultivate an intimate social relationship with its charges. The educated leaders especially assailed the indefinable political control of the district commissioner. In the latest stages an almost impossible task was given the Colonial Service, to dig its own grave by helping to rush through the transfer of power, and that into hands which it could not feel were ready, efficient, humane, or, always, uncorrupt.

You will hardly have failed to notice that I have said very little of the economic aspects of empire in our day. I have three pretty good reasons. First, I am not an economist. Second, the subject is vast and it is much more technical than the political aspect. Third, I believe that economic decisions depend more upon political decisions than vice-versa, above all perhaps in the context of empire. But I also believe that no serious economist would support the view held by the anti-colonialists, and perhaps especially by Africans, that Britain has immensely profited from plundering Africa's riches. The dramatic increases of production in most colonies have profited all concerned, the peasant producers and the metropolitan interests, while doubtless the expatriate trading companies have done pretty well, perhaps too well at certain times, from their two-way handling of the market. The researches of a specialist in this field, Professor Herbert Frankel, show that the return from minerals, up to the date of his enquiry in

1938, had not been unduly high as compared with profits in other parts of the world, when the risks and the costs of prospecting, developing, and redeveloping are subtracted.[1] It is probable that the profits and royalties from mining in certain areas since that date have been excessive, especially in view of the poverty of the native populations. But even though the economic motive was important and constant, Britain as a nation certainly did not build up her latest empire simply as a profitable investment: the biographies of the most active empire-builders and the colonial debates in Parliament give support to this view. Among many economic benefits required by the colonies was the security that allowed the infrastructure for future development to be laid. There is room for much research on the whole range of questions raised by this issue, and before critics make their easy assertion that Africa has been an El Dorado, they should do some pretty hard economic investigation and try to support their statement with figures.[2]

[1] H. S. Frankel: *Capital Investment in Africa* (London: Oxford University Press; 1938).

[2] An ambitious investigation, based on the figures, was attempted in 1936. It dealt with all the main modern colonial empires, and reached the general conclusion that these empires had been very

They should certainly read all that has been written in the West since Lenin's time on the theory of economic imperialism.

No record can ever be made of all that was accomplished, good, bad, and indifferent, by Britain in her dozen or more African territories during the brief years of her tenure. The mosaic is too vast for its pattern to be seen at one time or from one viewpoint, and we are always brought back to the question of standards by which to judge Britain's record. There can be no doubt, if the standard is to be the interests of the ruled, that these have steadily counted for more as the period of empire continued. The existence of informed liberal opinion, the publicity of debate, and the use of unofficial commissions of enquiry to probe every serious event and problem, all helped to this end. The African colonies, as the latest acquistions, have greatly benefited from the progression in virtue. Without doubt, especially in the latest years, as I have already explained, Britain was answering a demand from her subjects which she was finding it difficult to refuse, and nationalist leaders can con-

unprofitable enterprises to their rulers. Grover Clark: *The Balance Sheets of Imperialism* (New York: Columbia University Press; 1936).

163

gratulate themselves for forcing the pace. But much depends on the way concessions are made. Not only had Britain done much, though not, as I have admitted, enough in preparation, but through her agents she has worked to make the transfer of power as smooth and as helpful to the new states as she could. It is, indeed, amazing, and a tribute to both sides, that such great political changes have been carried out so far in these territories with so little bloodshed or even disorder.

There is another and embarrassing standard of judgement to which I must not shirk to refer—that set by the other modern colonial empires. Each colonial nation has had its own peculiar virtues and vices. I shall pay some tribute to the work of France in Negro Africa in my last lecture. Though both Belgium's and Holland's empires are not likely to be given rational assessment so long as the unhappy conclusions of their rule are uppermost in men's minds, the time will come when even historians of their once subject peoples will discover the attainments as well as the mistakes of their rule. I doubt whether the same will be done for Portugal, or for Italy, because of her wanton seizure of Ethiopia, though Italy certainly did much to redeem her record by her constructive work in Somalia during her tenure under the United Nations. This in some ways compared favourably with Britain's preparation of her part of Somaliland for independence. But over the whole record I am prepared to risk giving my opinion, which many impartial historians and observers have supported, that Britain on the whole was the most humane and considerate of modern colonial nations in Africa. It was, perhaps, fortunate that she was never tempted by the lure of wild rubber and other forest products to the terrific cruelties that marked the rule of King Leopold in the Congo and even that of the French in Equatorial Africa. It seems incontrovertible that she did most to prepare her subjects for self-government. These are no more than my own impressions from years of study and I am well aware that they will be regarded as biased.

Very recent events may have offered us some new standards of comparison and also made us realize the difficulties of annexing and pacifying what are now called underdeveloped peoples. The world has recently heard a little of how China has dealt with Tibet. We might think also of India's long struggle to reduce the Naga tribe to submission. Relevant, too, have been the measures that the United Nations, for all the purely idealistic aims of that organization, has employed to enforce its will upon the people of Katanga. Indeed many people, belonging to non-Western nations, who have been in the Congo Republic since its independence have come away with a wholly new appreciation of the difficulties of pacification and administration in Africa. We must hope that in the future African governments will show towards their own possible dissidents the high standard of humanity which they uphold in judging European rule.

I return to the point that, if Britain's record in Africa is to be understood, it is essential to have a comparative picture of the Africa Britain found and the Africa she is leaving. The African nationalism that I discussed in the second of my lectures tries to turn away from facing this old Africa. Yet, if, in the hope of placating this nationalism, we try to suppress or to forget the difficulties by which alone we can measure our achievements in Africa, we are only falsifying our own history—and with it the history of the new states themselves.

I cannot too often emphasize my belief, based on the most intimate experience of friendship and of academic teaching, in the inherent equality of

Africans. To enter into an equal friendship with an African is an adventure. Besides the joy of discovering another personality, of bridging the old, wide gap between the races, one learns the essential oneness of humanity, with a new quality, that of the African inheritance, added. Even before the time when such relationships were possible, within the limited but virile setting of tribal life, Africans have shown nearly all the range of human qualities. I have sat by a camp-fire in what would be regarded as the most primitive part of Africa and I have seen the twilight play on the faces of the old men, finely carved by experience—this one might well have been a judge, that one a bishop, the one beyond quite evidently the local humorist. The record of that courageous and lone explorer, Mungo Park, bears witness to the kindness of Negro women to a passing stranger too poor to reward them. I know, too, that through archaeology and anthropology, and the piecing together of old records by a young and able group of British scholars, a new picture is being built up today of the Africa of the past.[3] But I must also think of the records of the first travellers in many—not all—

[3] There are two books which summarize the evidence, written with the strong aim of correcting a too depreciatory view of Africa's past, by Basil Davidson: *Old Africa Rediscovered* (London:

parts of the continent, the stories of my old pioneer friends, even my own first contacts some thirty years ago. All those combine into a picture. Alongside the joys of the dance, the drum, the hunt, the beer-drink, the picture is dark with poverty, ignorance, hunger, disease, isolation, cruelty, human sacrifice, even cannibalism. These evils are not yet wholly conquered.

In the context of the old Africa it could be argued that they were not evils, at least not moral evils. But there is no educated African today who does not want to see them ended and, if possible, forgotten. Could the changes he so much welcomes have been achieved so quickly, in a period when there was no international agency to attempt the task, except by the more humane European nations? Much that Africa needed from the world has been given, some of it freely and at great cost, for Africa is very hard to serve.

Before we draw up our final account one further point should not be forgotten. Once the white man had entered Africa, one might almost say

---

Victor Gollancz; 1959) and *Black Mother* (London: Victor Gollancz; 1961). Readers who wish to follow up this important point can do so in *The Journal of African History*, ed. R. A. Olliver and J. D. Fage (Cambridge: Cambridge University Press).

once his modern rifle had reached Africa, the option was no longer between the old freedom and
the new colonial rule. It was between that rule
and anarchy. Read the ghastly story of the Arab
slave trade on the eve of European annexation, or
of the murderous raiding that pierced into the regions of the Upper Nile from Egypt and the Sudan. It was the same tale in Africa as in the first
European contacts with the Maoris and the Poly-
nesians. Albert Schweitzer wrote—and he should
know: "The independence of the primitive is lost
at the moment when the first white man's boat
arrives with powder or rum, salt or fabrics."
Government, with all its faults, was a thousand
times better than the unregulated contact of men,
white, brown, or black, armed with terrible power
to corrupt or destroy. Britain's record is mixed.
She could be slow, neglectful, unimaginative. She
might, however, have done much more if the sudden growth of African nationalism had not prematurely cut short her slow and steady work on the
foundations of the new states. Once that had happened, she could only say, as when a father begins
to build a model construction toy with his children, and is suddenly called away: "Look—here
are the rest of the pieces. I cannot do any more.

Build it yourselves in your own way." The simile has some value, though the Africans, of course, are not children. They will use the materials of the West, but they will use them in their own way and will add more, much more, of their own creation. Above all, they alone can provide the dynamo of nationalism which will make the model work.

V I

The Prospect

In ASSESSING the British colonial record in these talks I have drawn my examples mainly from British dependencies and mainly from their political aspects in the past and present. When we turn to consider the future of these states, as they take their independent place in a largely independent continent, our horizon widens. Under colonial rule each state was isolated from its neighbours to an extraordinary degree: nearly all its relations were with the imperial power. Now, suddenly, each state has to look at the frontiers for which it is responsible, get on co-operative terms with its neighbours, and look beyond them to the future of Africa as a whole and of the world in general. In this last talk I want to follow this widening and forward view.

I have described how the realization by the small educated and travelled élites of the inferior status of their race in the world goaded them to find dignity, as much as freedom, in political independence. Some of their hopes have already come true. To the world at large, until very recent years, Africans remained mere figures in census reports or labour statistics. A few names reached the history books or the newspapers, that of the Zulu tyrant Chaka; of Moshesh of Basutoland; of the Khamas, father, son, and grandson; of Dr. Aggrey. Now the names of Africa's leaders figure in newspapers and are heard on the radio; their faces appear on television as they fly about the world on high political matters. The world has revised its attitudes and adjusted its manners now that it has to deal with presidents living in palaces and ministers allotting contracts of millions of pounds.

Yet the leaders carry over into the new dimension of freedom much of the old passionate anticolonialism. One reason is that, though they are now politically free, they are still the prisoners of their own weakness and poverty. The historian

172

Gibbon said of Ethiopia that, after its contact with the Roman Empire and with Christianity, it went to sleep for a thousand years. Most of tropical Africa lay in this sleep of isolation for all the thousands of history's years. Sixty years of even the most effective colonial rule in the most favourable regions has not gone far to equip Africans to take as yet anything like an equal place with other nations in the modern world.

It is unlikely that they will be allowed to go to sleep again. They have awoken into a strangely situated world which offers them a political compensation for their physical weakness. Because of the apparent equality of power between the free world and the Communist states, and because the nature of modern war is such that it is almost impossible to wage it, the so-called third, or uncommitted, world holds a balancing position out of all proportion to its military strength. This third world consists largely of ex-colonial states, and now the twenty-eight new African states come crowding in to join their older African neighbours, Ethiopia, Egypt, and Liberia. Eleven of these new states have less than three million inhabitants: some of them have only a million or less, but the vote of each counts as much as the vote of the United States, Russia, or Britain. Here is a fantastic discrepancy between legal status and real power. How serious are its results? Is there perhaps even some advantage in having a kind of detached, neutral jury who cast their votes according to their main objectives? These are to attack the remaining strongholds of colonialism; to ban war and, above all, the atomic weapons; and to induce the rich powers to direct to their own empty coffers the wealth they are pouring into armaments.

Sir Andrew Cohen, who was permanent British representative at UNO from 1953 to 1961 and has therefore had a ringside seat, has said that there the Western powers have suffered little from the strange distribution of voting power and that Russia has suffered more, especially over the Congo problem.[1] The reason is that the small states regard the United Nations as the main safeguard for their sovereignty, for their rights, and indeed almost for their existence. Aid that comes to them through the United Nations loses its strings on the way. Whereas some of the Western powers have in some measure accepted this situation, it would cut right across Russia's techniques of direct action. Her attitude towards both the office and the person of Mr. Hammarskjöld, whom the small

[1] Sir A. Cohen: "The New Africa and the United Nations," *African Affairs*, October 1961.

states regarded as their champion, threw them solidly against Russia in September 1960.

So long as the world's balance hangs so evenly, and has to be maintained, short of war, by rather misnamed diplomatic methods, then so long will the neutrals hold their make-weight power. The African states are certainly fortunate in the date of their birth as the very existence of UNO offers them a great international auditorium where the smallest power can make a resounding speech to the world, and where the poorest power, which cannot afford much in the way of embassies, can conduct its foreign affairs in the lobbies.

But the more deeply we look into the world situation, the less able are we to be optimistic about the results of bringing this mass of small powers to birth. All states want to ban war—except when they can find no other way of achieving the ends nearest their interests or their safety. It already appears that in pursuit of their major aim the anti-colonialist states regard armed force, revolution, and even war as legitimate methods. So long as the world's nations cannot bring themselves to give the United Nations both the international principles and the power to achieve peaceful change, so long will states resort to national violence. The major Western powers have never been able, partly because of the great division in the world, to rely upon international action to protect their interests, and they have therefore had to shift their stance from power to law, as occasion seemed to demand, in a way that has laid them open to the accusation of inconsistency and even hypocrisy. It is therefore easy enough for the large company of small new states, who have their deep bias against Western domination, to condemn these powers. Few, indeed, of the world's nations have clean records. Britain, France, and America have all lately resorted to private war to try to protect their interests. The records of Germany and Italy over the last few decades hardly qualify them for moral leadership, and the Communist states could not even begin to compete for it. Yet the struggle for the difficult ideal of international law and action must go on if the world is not to slide into complete anarchy. It is therefore important that the Western powers should understand both the character and the strength of the anti-colonial passion which unites the majority of the world's states against them, those states which, because of their weakness and their needs, could be the keenest supporters of the United Nations. To understand, and as far as possible to assuage this passion—the African manifestation of which I have tried to interpret—is a pressing need for the Western powers, and one in which Britain is well qualified to play an important part.

But the young African states are at least learning that they are no more immune than the wicked old nations from the international evils of frontier disputes and irredentism, nor even from the ideological differences that have led to groups being called by the names of the different capitals in which they confer. Not even on the Congo collapse, with its humiliating horrors and its threat of bringing the cold war into the heart of Africa, could the new independent states act in unison. And what hard choices are presented to them! Dr. Nkrumah entered into helpful economic relations with Israel—a country so well qualified to offer assistance to Africa—but he found at the Casablanca Conference that he had to join with Egypt in condemning his friend as a neo-colonialist tool of the West. How embarrassing at the African conference table to have to confront Ethiopia and Somalia with their envenomed frontier dispute! How hard, too, for new rulers, who dreamed perhaps of Pan-Africa, or even of West African federation, to abandon the shining new power and honour of complete sovereign independence! It is surely the obligation as well as the interest of the Western powers, and especially of their former rulers, to help these new nations overcome their differences and co-operate and where possible federate into larger units that will give Africa strength at home and abroad.

The new states take over, of course, the legacy of division left by the colonial powers. West Africa, especially, was shared out by France and Britain in a most haphazard way. The powers differed in so much more than language. How strange to see the cultural differences between the two nations mirrored on the broken surface of Africa! France consciously took up the torch of Rome. Her faith was in universal human reason and in unity through government, law, and culture, and she tried to hold all her colonies within the embrace of a greater France. But African nationalism was strong enough to demand her sudden and complete surrender to the same independence and fragmentation that were the end product of Britain's very different policy. But for France and for her colonies the past may prove to be not all lost. Again like Rome, France called her provincials to the councils in her capital, and many of the new African leaders learned high-level politics in equal association with Frenchmen in Paris, an advantage that no leaders in ex-British Africa can match.

But in the former British colonies there are
many more Africans than in the ex-French colonies
who have had experience in handling local affairs
at different levels, from the quasi-parliaments of
legislative councils down to tribal chieftainship
and councils. France, with her ideas of centraliza-
tion and her belief in equality, had little respect for
tribal hierarchy and custom. I remember once going from Nigeria, where one could hardly obtain
an audience with the emir in his spreading palace,
into French territory just across the border. Here I
was sent to see the local emir, once the peer of his
Nigerian neighbour. The interpreter sat outside
sounding the horn of our car until the emir came
running obediently out of his crumbling quarters.
But, to give the other side, on the southern rim of
the Sahara I met one of the veiled Tuareg with his
camels, and tried to learn his opinion of French
administration. "But, madame!" he said, drawing
himself up to the height of his slender, wiry frame,
"I am a French citizen."

This is France's old magic, her power to give
herself to those who could reach up to accept the
gift. Long ago, in mid-eighteenth century North
America, our own agent with the Red Indians, Sir
William Johnson, exclaimed in jealous admiration
that only the French could prove that an Indian

hunter could become a civilized member of society. This secret weapon of assimilation stands France in good stead today. Nearly all her West African states keep their social and economic links with her, and this even while she continues to fight her Algerian rebels, who presented too hard an Islamic surface for her assimilative influences to pierce. Most of her former Negro provinces, now small independent states, are bound by need to accept the generous help she gives them in staff and economic privileges, and her outstanding assistance in finance. But, even if all these ties should fray or break, even though Guinea and Mali have struck their independent attitudes, it seems certain that what was French Negro Africa will long retain the deep intelligible pattern of French influence. This is because, with all her mistakes, she gave the African élite what they valued more than anything else in the world, what we so long failed to give them, the respect of equality. If ex-British and ex-French Africa could enter into some form of confederation, fusing English and French influences with their own rich native variety of cultures, West Africa might in time—a long time—become one of the world's leading states.

The Africans of the former French and British colonies look out on the ex-Belgian Congo, a sight bitter to African hope and pride, for it reveals not only Belgium's great miscalculation, but also what Africa can still be without adequate help from the outside world. Farther south the prospect is much easier for them to judge. South Africa and the Portuguese colonies exhibit the unyielding supremacy of white over black. While these situations exist they can be condemned utterly, and all colonialism, past and present, can, when occasion demands, be associated with their condemnation. And all Western policy will also be condemned for tolerating them, while Communist propaganda is given its maximum opportunity.

Portugal claims that her policy is one of racial equality and that she has given freely of her blood in race mixture. She has, indeed, helped breed a large new Christian nation with an incalculably great future in Brazil, and a small Christian community in Goa, whose emigrants to East Africa, some of whom I know well, have won the highest character. But in Angola and Mozambique she has done little to gain acquittal from the charge of colonialism in its severest form. The Africans there are too numerous and too solidly different for her to endow them fully with her blood. The records of our Anti-Slavery Society would show the efforts over a long series of years to expose Portugal's way

with her African labour, and there was a time
when British governments and public men were
active in protest. But the way that may lead from
Portuguese province to African nation is not likely
to be quick or easy. The lesson of the Congo disaster is clear. Until the United Nations is able to
offer strong, continuous, and constructive help to
an African state, as it emerges unprepared, and
perhaps rebelliously, out of colonial rule, the alternative to colonialism may well be anarchy.

What of South Africa? Here is what may be
the last beleaguered stronghold of white mastery in
Africa. Its ruling garrison are Africans, white Africans, who will defend their position to the last, for
they are, in fact, a little nation that has built itself
over three centuries into this position and has nowhere else to go. They have their backs to the wall,
but they dare not turn to read the writing on it.
Yet the rest of the world can read it. Their state
rests upon the foundation of absolute power over
the black population. Their economic and social
subordination is maintained by a network of legal
discrimination which binds ten million people so
tightly that not one, not the most educated or able,
can escape to freedom or equality—unless, indeed,
he manages to escape the country. Most of the
main opposition party are British, once the masters,

but now reduced to near impotence by the growth of the Afrikaner in numbers, political skill, and resolution and also by their own fear of the subordinated Africans, which is greater than their fear of the Afrikaners. Yet they, and especially the large business element they contain, exercise in practice some liberalizing influence. The real heroes of the stronghold are those who, although their lives are committed to the country, maintain against immense odds the struggle for justice for the black Africans.

Yet South Africa is not quite all it seems to the outside world, especially perhaps to its outside African critics. Certainly the government's controls cut harshly into the sensitivities of human nature and the bonds of family life. Yet many of the Africans have a level of wages, housing, schooling, medical care, and other amenities far higher than that of the great majority of Africans to the north. On my last visit to the native locations of Johannesburg I could burn with indignation to see the bulldozers destroying the cherished African freehold location of Sophiatown. But, nearby I could remark in the new location the improved, if dreary housing, and the healthy look of the children, especially of the hundreds of little girls playing in their neat gym tunics.

183

Some of the tribes have now lived for nearly three centuries within a European-conducted state, with all that involves in the way of sophistication as well as subordination. They have been built in, as it were, if only at the bottom grade, to the richest and most highly developed economy in Africa. As long as they have any hope they will want to infiltrate upwards from within the citadel. They may therefore not be wholly responsive to the cries of those outside, or even of the most uncompromising of their own leaders, whose impatient voices seem to call upon them to blow it up, and who will certainly be offered the necessary dynamite by the Communists. True, the system is a defiance of all accepted economic laws—as is the absurd policy of so-called Bantustan—but economic laws have a way of ultimately asserting themselves. This needs time, however, and time may not be allowed to South Africa. Yet, if the Africans did succeed one day in taking over the state unharmed, they might constitute the richest state in Africa. Disciplined by adversity, their own culture deeply imprinted by Western civilization, they might stand at some point between the Negroes of Africa and those of the New World, who, like them, are the products of different kinds of slavery and subjection.

Before we turn away from the Portuguese and South African states, we must remember that we have to conduct a policy towards them. This policy will be the main test applied to us by the colonial world. The African leaders in the Union say to us what one actually said to me the other day: "What are you going to do to help us? Have we got to face our grim struggle without any help or encouragement from you? We know we can get it from the other side, but we would still prefer to keep out of their hands." The nationalist government in South Africa congratulates itself that British and American financial elements have such an interest in the Union as a stable sphere for investment that their governments can be trusted to do nothing that will upset the status quo. The Portuguese government, in some measure, may perhaps aspire to this same satisfaction. Are we as a nation content to go on drawing profit from countries where there is no freedom for the labour that does so much to produce it, without using our utmost influence upon the two governments to persuade them to reform this helotry? In South Africa, even if we did not have three hostages in the High Commission territories, we could not congratulate ourselves that we have disposed of our difficult relations with the Union by bowing her out of the commonwealth. The test the anti-colonial world will apply to us is our policy towards the states of southern Africa south of a line of about ten degrees.

I am not suggesting that the decisions will be rosy. I know that we have solid interests as well as liberal principles. I know that the government of a nation regards it as its first duty to survive, and that we are not as strong as we were when we gave effective moral support to peoples in South America, Italy, and elsewhere, who in Gladstone's phrase were "rightly struggling to be free." But today we have a very strong partner who is committed to the cause of freedom, and we can surely work wholeheartedly with America in showing that there are forces in the West biased in favour of colonial freedom with as much strength as those of Communism, but rather more principle and judgement.

As Britain and France step back to the sidelines, the United States steps forward to join them there. This new presence—let us confess it—was not at first easy for Britain to accept. It seemed sometimes as if Americans were saying to the Africans, even while Britain was engaged in the final delicate transfer of power: "*We* understand the meaning of freedom. We wrested it ourselves from these same colonialists, and once we have cleared away the last relics of British control, we can get down to the real business of helping you."

If some individuals *did* give this impression, they did injustice to their nation as a whole. America, like other nations, includes brash young nationalists and hard-faced businessmen. But she has been ready to put her great wealth into the service of the world as no other nation has ever done. She has bred specialists, indeed statesmen, in philanthropy who have so committed themselves to this complex, world-wide business of international aid that they have almost forgotten any particular American interest. America's concern with Africa came late, but, characteristically, she has made a remarkably quick start. A very few years ago the evidences of American concern with Africa could have been listed in a brief pamphlet: today a fat volume would be needed. It would include the many activities of the government itself, its diplomacy, its complex machinery for aid and service, the great philanthropic trusts, the universities, the business world, the Christian missions, and many more facets of American life that are now turned towards Africa.

Americans are in a hurry; so are Africans. So ought *we* to be. Moreover, America's unavoidable ignorance is being repaired—also at America's pace! In recent years I have had to do with a stream of her young graduates. They take post-graduate degrees in Oxford en route to Africa, and I am deeply impressed by their intelligence and enthusiasm. Major studies are now coming from the new African departments in American universities. Some of them strike a new line, probing deeply and theoretically into the nature of African politics. And how generously American funds have been given to us to help our own African and, indeed, our other studies! I certainly should not forget this generosity, for my own college has been greatly helped by them and thus my own work has been assisted. With her great resources, her idealism and belief in freedom, America is certain to take a great, perhaps the greatest, part in giving to Africa the help that Africa needs.

Confronting America, and also reaching out to Africa, stand Russia and her satellite powers, joining in the struggle to win the minds of the non-Western world. The achievement of independence lays Africa's new states wide open not only to the influence, but now to the activities, of the Communist states. The colonial powers used their authority to put up barriers against this influence. The inevitable response of the awakening African nationalists was: "If *you* are so much against Com-

munism, there clearly must be something in it for
us." And they found something—the practical example of Russia's rapid advance in industry, agriculture, and education. They were struck, too, by
the absolute racial equality that Russia preaches
and is believed to practise in her vast empire, though
there race is a minor problem.

The Communists have at least two potential
holds over the young African states. One concerns
the matter of economic aid, and with this I shall
deal in a moment. The other is education. Africans' thirst for education is such that they would
accept it from the devil himself. So an ever increasing stream of students flows into Russia. There
they first learn the language and then spend several
years at colleges or universities. A Peoples' Friendship University, significantly renamed the Lumumba University, has been established in Moscow. It offers long courses of training, ultimately
to 4,000 students, many of whom will be Africans.
To counter Russia's own ignorance, serious research work on African sociology and history is
now being carried out at Moscow and Leningrad
universities—and need I add that African history
is being rewritten? [2] Meanwhile, Russia and the

[2] Mary Holdsworth: "African Studies in the U.S.S.R.," *African
Affairs*, Saint Antony's Papers, No. 10 (London: Chatto & Windus; 1961), pp. 89-101.

satellite states direct upon Africans, and especially young Africans and trade unionists, a spreading complex of agencies.

What are their chances of success? So far it is estimated that of the world's 40,000,000 Communists only about 50,000 are in Africa, and these mostly in the extreme north and south. Communists, indeed, are somewhat baffled by their failure to find in Africa—at least outside South Africa— the necessary stage-setting within which to play out the implacable drama of their revolution. Where is the dispossessed, land-hungry peasantry? Too few, too localized. The urban proletariat? Too few, again; too embryonic. The bourgeoisie, ripe for liquidation? Too few in most regions; too essential in others. Some revolutions, yes—but mostly such peaceful revolutions! With many of the expected Marxist necessities absent, some very improper elements are strongly present: racialism, nationalism, tribalism, and, surely, not a little personality cult. Among pagan, Christian, and Moslem there is also a deep belief in another world which makes them allergic to any anti-God campaign. And remember that on a map of religions Islam can be shown coming down over the great shoulders of Africa like a cape. Perhaps the strongest obstacle to Communism is something I have emphasized in all these talks, the passion of Africans to escape from all subjection. They are therefore determined not to get rid of the domination of one set of white men only to fall under that of another.

The Communist theorists are troubled by all this, but not dismayed. They can wait. They believe that in time the developments which their theory demands will, indeed must, come about and then what they call scientific socialism will swallow up all these regrettable errors.

Does it seem strange to us that Africans should appear to be so open to influence from a state which has not allowed a single of its own many dependencies to escape its power, which has bloodily repressed any "nationalist" stirrings, deported whole peoples, and in some places planted new lands with Russian settlers? It should *not* seem strange. The Africans are still held in the emotions of their revolt against the power and influence of the West. It is from *that* standpoint that they look out upon the world. For them the light falls on Russia's challenge to the West; Russia's offers of help; her achievements; her purposeful energy. The darker sides both of theory and of practice still lie in the shadow.

China stands beside Russia here. She, too, is stepping up every sort of activity in Africa: offering education, including that in guerrilla warfare; sending experts and entertainers; and diffusing a growing volume of influence by radio. She has some advantages over Russia. She suffered herself at the hands of the imperialists. And she has carried out an amazingly thorough communist revolution through her peasantry. Moreover, her people can be regarded as coloured—at least they are not white.

There is also the matter of economic aid. The subject is a jungle of facts and figures, of changing theories and difficult practices. I must skirt around it. One thing is clear. Africa is going to make an immense demand on the rest of the world. A dangerous discrepancy yawns between the hopes of Africans and their capacity to attain them. The Western nations increased their own wealth and their skills —the two are really indivisible—over many years during which governments, under capitalist influence, were able to impose under-consumption on the masses. The sudden wholesale enfranchisement of the poor and inexperienced masses in Africa makes that discipline impossible there—even if we wished to see it repeated. What then? The capital must be supplied from outside? But Africa no longer offers the security that enabled colonial governments to obtain a flow of capital. Will the Western

powers therefore make adequate, steadily maintained financial sacrifices for political ends?

It is on this economic side that the Communist
states have their greatest opportunity. They control
all their own economic forces and can deploy them
when and where they will. The new African leaders rule people of immense poverty and immense
expectations. A population graph will show a
mounting line while the agricultural price index,
unless the Western powers can help to stabilize it,
will zigzag dangerously. Popular disappointment,
tribal disunity, and other difficulties may tempt
African governments to increasingly dictatorial
methods. If so, Communist tutors will be ready to
show them their techniques of control. More likely,
the Communists will direct against the old leaders
the impatient young men as these return a few
years hence from Marxist academies.

Mr. George Kennan has warned us that we must
learn to live in the same world as the Communist
states and that we should not exaggerate their
danger to us. We liberal British long to heed this
warning because we hate to feel obliged to hate.
Even in the universities our theoretical studies get
tainted with the inescapable obsession of anti-Com-
munism. It must therefore be our hope that time
will blunt the dangerous sharpness of the ideological

division, and that no consortium of Communist
states will now pass the Africans through their iron
mill and turn them out docile, unified, literate, reasonably productive, but with their minds sealed
against the West. We may hope that Africa will obtain donations of steel mills from Russia and will
learn rice-growing from the Chinese without having
to pay the full political price: that the difficulty of
helping Africa may teach moderation even to Communists, or that inter-Communist rifts may weaken
their offensive. But we cannot sit back and *hope*
that this will happen and that Africa will retain our
gradualist and liberal traditions, or return to them.
The struggle being waged in Europe and Asia and
South America is only now being extended to this
fourth continent. Disunity, poverty, and inexperience make Negro Africa a vulnerable region. And
in South Africa it exposes a tempting Achilles' heel.

On our side, we shall not find the African states
easy to help. They ask, indeed demand, financial
aid from their rich but hesitant suitors while they
remain determined in no way to compromise their
political chastity in return. The aid they accept
must not even bear the moral taint of philanthropy.

It may be that in these talks I have erred on
the side of pessimism. Not that I would take back

any of the fears I have voiced. But perhaps we should allow a little more for that incalculable factor, human nature. Africa, or parts of it, may yet surprise us. African human nature is undergoing a crisis. It is not enough for Africa's peoples, as it is not enough for any peoples dominated by the West, to escape from Western political power. The crushed mind and the wounded dignity have to recover. As we have seen in Asia, there are three possible reactions. One, generally the first, is for subjected peoples to try to reach out with both hands to appropriate the new Western model. This early reaction has often bred a small generation of those who have thus been assimilated. When the Western presence withdraws and the forces of nationalism advance, this generation may find itself stranded and lonely between the two forces. A second reaction is to reject the West, to endeavour to revive and assert the native culture, and especially, where possible, its religion. The third possibility is to attempt a synthesis of the two, not only—as is almost unavoidable—at the more superficial level, but at the deepest level of religion and philosophy, a task of the greatest difficulty and value. In this task the Indians have given the lead, and they have benefited, as other peoples can also, from the Western scholarship which has done so much to recover the literature and art of their past.

Africans are divided between the first two attitudes to which I have just referred. But, perhaps, at the moment, they feel most the desire to reassert their old ethos and develop new riches out of it. Their task is obviously much more difficult for them than theirs was for the Asians. The Africans' fierce reaction from the world's scorn or neglect demands that this African personality should be unique. This was, at least in its first manifestations, a sophisticated reaction; and significantly, it was the gallicized Africans of the Caribbean and Africa who coined the word *négritude* and developed the idea of a special African personality behind the word.

Africa has already given some new things to the world. West African sculpture deeply impressed and indeed influenced Western Europe with its combination of rude earthiness and extreme stylization. It sometimes contains an element of horror, as if it spoke of cruelty and black magic in the dark rain forests. Painting is a new technique: Africans, however, already show an amazing power to pour out their world of rich fantasy and tropical colour on to canvas. But Africa is, above all, the continent of the dance. As I look back over my travels, I seem to feel Africa's lands throbbing under millions of bare, stamping feet, with swaying, sweating bodies above them. Inseparable from the dance is the broken rhythm of the drum. These married arts have come to Europe by way of the slaves of the New World, and it is characteristic of Africans that even out of slavery they could distil joy. Jazz and its large off-spring of rhythm and dance have captured America and Europe. Africa knew how to use the synco-pated magic of the drum to summon ecstacy, even unconsciousness, and perhaps, in the abandon-ment of our youth to this spell, she inflicts a subtle revenge!

In literature, also, Africans have shown their power, above all to reveal in their novels and poems both the extreme of frustration and the capacity for adjustment which their racial experi-ence evokes. In all these ways the Negro race has offered new enrichment to the culture of the world. And this is only a beginning.[3]

While we think of the energy and joyousness that so many Africans possess, I must share with you a more personal impression. I have discussed

[3] An interesting discussion of this subject will be found in Jan-heinz Jahn: *Muntu, an Outline of Neo-African Cultures* (Lon-don: Faber & Faber; 1961).

the many problems of the transfer of power, and they are real enough. But when I was invited by the governments of Somalia and Nigeria in 1960 to share their birthday celebrations, I was able to appreciate the wealth of joy and pride released by the event. The Somalis in their desert poverty, the Nigerians in their vast numbers, with their immense possibilities, brimmed over with happiness, breaking into song and dance and overwhelming their European visitors with the warmth of their welcome. When in Nigeria, at midnight on October 1, before the vast crowds on Lagos race course I saw the Union Jack flutter down the post, I felt a wholly unexpected, almost physical shock. It may have been that, having made some study of Nigeria's history, I realized just what it was that was being brought to an end, all the hopes and fears, the achievements and mistakes, the work of hundreds of British lives, many of which ended in this country. But immediately the Nigerian flag ran up, and the assembled Nigerians of all regions and tribes saluted it with unmeasured pride and hope. I realized then that, whatever our regrets or forebodings, the incalculable force of human energy and pride would be harnessed behind the new nation.

This brings me back, after wandering far, to

the question in my first talk. What are likely to
be Britain's relations with her former subjects?
There is much we still share: the Queen, if not the
Crown; the English language; the great gift of our
law and procedure; and the ideals, at least, of our
pattern of democracy. There is the enlivening link
between our universities, if we can adjust our traditions to their needs and work closely with the
Americans who are now entering this field with
their wealth of experience and money. These and
our many other bonds could weaken, but there are
new ones which we can still create. Much will depend upon our dealings here in Britain with many
thousands of often lonely African students and, on
the other side, upon the readiness of our young
doctors, lawyers, scientists, and above all, teachers
of every kind to go out for at least two or three
years to serve the great needs of Africa in the
spirit that Africa now demands. This, in turn, re-
quires that those who hold authority in Britain
should facilitate such ventures, perhaps by second-
ment, and make them a qualification in a career
and not the reverse.

The atmosphere in Britain may not seem propitious for vision or sacrifices. But both exist out
of the headlines. The statistics of empire do not
record the uncovenanted mercies that have accom-

panied it and we seldom refer to such things. I am thinking now of those who have achieved what I have never attempted—those who have given an unostentatious working lifetime to the service of Africa. Think especially of that immense army of missionaries which went out, often before any government or security, to lay the foundations of the Christian faith and of Western education, the greatest gifts of all the West had to offer. There are at this moment some 20,000 missionaries from all the churches serving quietly in Africa. They face, at the deepest level, the struggle in the soul of Africans between their new faith and their self-assertion against what seems, however wrongly, to be the white man's religion. For an African, as for a European, to be a true Christian in the Africa of today is to accept a deeply sacrificial life.

Behind Britain today lies wealth, power, and empire. Before her, still wealth perhaps, but also a difficult choice of directions. Whichever we choose, we must try to keep, indeed to increase, what are perhaps our two main assets, our great knowledge of the peoples of the former empire and the measure of understanding and good will we share with them. The knowledge will have to be fostered in our universities and in other ways. The good will may even, in time, outgrow anti-colonialism, as it has to a considerable extent in India. I would indeed say here how grateful we should be for the historical understanding and even appreciation we have had from many Indian writers and thinkers. For, after all, we too have our feelings, our hidden nationalism; we are not political eunuchs.

We cannot, I believe, use such residual assets of empire as remain to us in a vain attempt to rebuild some kind of independent assertive or arbitral power in the world. But there are still many ways in which we can give direct help to Africa, or join with our American and European allies in supplying aid. In spite of all the difficulties and disappointments that have accompanied recent enterprises of the United Nations, I most firmly believe that our greatest contribution would be to put all our strength and experience behind the international organs in which alone lies the possibility of peace and mutual help. The younger generation is most likely to be able to make the adjustment from national power to international service. The young can also share with Africans an immense capacity for happiness, a love of sport, and the joy and energy that has shown itself in the dancing and the music and has carried them through their poverty and enslavement. Policy for Africa is, of course, only one part of our whole external policy. What we do abroad can be an extension only of what we are at home, of our success in showing that our free institutions can still help us solve our many domestic problems. Yet, equally, our welfare state cannot succeed without a humane and alert adjustment to a rapidly changing world—and no part is changing more quickly than Africa.

Giving direct help is expensive in effort and money, but it presents less difficult issues than those of forcign policy. The whole ex-colonial world, so strong and united in its anti-colonialism, so weak as yet in its effective strength in the concrete terms of economic and military power, looks to us for a more consistent and sympathetic response than we have hitherto given. Our military necessities, our economic interests, perhaps our historic prejudices, seem to result in an equivocal policy on the issues that so greatly concern these nations. They are no longer interested in our reiteration of how many peoples we *have* freed; they await our future dealings with both the newly freed and the still unfree. We have no longer the independent strength that enabled us to give effective encouragement to peoples in South America, Italy, and elsewhere who in Gladstone's phrase were "rightly struggling to be free." But in America we have a strong ally who is committed to the support of freedom, and the time has surely arrived when we must work with her to show more clearly that the Western belief in freedom is as strong as that of the Communists in their theories, and much more disinterested.

In making my colonial reckoning I have thought of myself in the main as speaking to my own people. Few Africans are ready to rationalize about our record or their own, still less to appreciate the services of colonialism. Their present mood is to give up being grateful, or humble, or afraid, or ashamed, or even impressed. They have had so much of all that. They are determined to be something quite new—Africans! And impress us! When we talk to them about politics—it is a pity we talk of so little else—they answer from the blood and not from the brain, projecting upon us the difficulties that arise from deep historical causes for which neither they nor we are responsible. This projection may continue until they confront these causes and we cease to regard black as the colour of inferiority. Immense difficulties face the new states through which Africans intend to assert their equality. It may be a very long time before they succeed in this. The lamps of Africa may go out even before they are alight, as some of the lamps of Europe have gone out. Whether they do or not will depend very much upon the degree of understanding and help which we in the West give to Africa during the next two or three critical years.

Index

A NOTE ABOUT THE AUTHOR

MARGERY FREDA PERHAM was born in 1895 in Lancashire, England. She attended St. Anne's School, Abbots Bromley; St. Stephens College, Windsor; and St. Hugh's College, Oxford. She began her professional career as an assistant lecturer in history at Sheffield University. Then, after a year in Somaliland (1922-3), she was Fellow and Tutor in Modern History and "Modern Greats" at St. Hugh's College, Oxford (1924-9). In 1931-2 she went around the world on a Rhodes Traveling Fellowship to study the administration of colored races in North America, Polynesia, Australia, and Africa. The next year took her to West Africa, and she has made frequent visits to Africa and the West Indies since. She has been a Research Fellow of St. Hugh's College (1930-9); Reader in Colonial Administration at Oxford (1939-48); Director of Oxford University Institute of Colonial Studies (1945-8); Fellow in Imperial Government, Nuffield College, Oxford, since 1947. Miss Perham was named a Commander of the British Empire in 1948; awarded an honorary doctorate of laws by St. Andrews University in 1952; elected a Fellow of the British Academy in 1961. Her publications include *Native Administration in Nigeria* (1937), *Race and Politics in Kenya* (with Elspeth Huxley, 1944), *Lugard* (two volumes, 1956, 1960), *The Diaries of Lord Lugard* (with Mary Bull, 1959), *African Discovery* (with J. Simmons, 1948), *The Government of Ethiopia* (1948), as well as two early novels. She has edited a series, *Colonial and Comparative Studies,* published by Faber and Faber (1948), which includes several studies of colonial legislatures, and a two-volume study of Nigerian economics, *Economics of a Tropical Dependency* (1948). She has also contributed to such American publications as *The New York Times* and *Foreign Affairs.* Miss Perham lives in Nuffield College, Oxford, England, where she is Senior Fellow and the only woman Official Fellow in the one mixed college in Oxford. She is on the Executive Committee of the Inter-University Council for Higher Education Overseas.

A NOTE ON THE TYPE

THE TEXT of this book is set in Electra, a Linotype face designed by W. A. Dwiggins (1880-1956). This face cannot be classified as either modern or old-style. It is not based on any historical model, nor does it echo any particular period or style. It avoids the extreme contrasts between thick and thin elements that mark most modern faces, and attempts to give a feeling of fluidity, power, and speed.

Composed, printed, and bound by
H. Wolff, New York.
Typography and binding design by
VINCENT TORRE